—

"*Sesame* opens up a world of possibilities for delicious, inspired cooking and baking using one of my favorite kitchen essentials. Rachel brings joy, passion, and style to every page of this cookbook, which will become as much of a staple as sesame itself."

—**Adeena Sussman**, food writer and *New York Times* bestselling author

"As a tahini enthusiast, I could not wait to get my hands on this book! It is both inspiring and drool-worthy, and I loved learning more about sesame. I can't wait to make every recipe!"

—**Melissa Ben-Ishay**, founder of Baked by Melissa and author of *Come Hungry*

"Seed + Mill's tahini is a mainstay in my cabinet, and a tahini soft serve at their Chelsea Market shop is an unmissable stop in New York. I am inspired by Rachel's dedication to celebrating and sharing this ancient seed with the world through her delicious creations and can't wait to add this quintessential cookbook to my collection."

—**Jing Gao**, chef, entrepreneur, and author of *The Book of Sichuan Chili Crisp*

"I'm such a huge fan of Seed + Mill, and Rachel Simons has showcased the ways the simple sesame seed is a gastronomically delicious food in *Sesame* (not to mention that tahini is a superfood and great for your skin). These mouthwatering recipes jump off the page, and they're so simple that even a non-chef like me can re-create them."

—**Bobbi Brown**, entrepreneur, author, podcast host, and founder of Bobbi Brown Cosmetics and Jones Road Beauty

T0349342

# RACHEL SIMONS

FOUNDER OF SEED + MILL

# SESAME

GLOBAL RECIPES & STORIES OF AN ANCIENT SEED

Photography by Alan Benson
Illustrations by Evelina Edens
Additional text by Maren Ellingboe King

TEN SPEED PRESS
California | New York

*For my mum, Jane, and my grandparents, Otto and Annika.*

*For teaching me to plant seeds, but also empowering me to hitch a ride with the wind, scattering some of those seeds to far and distant places.*

With my grandfather, Otto, in his garden in Bulawayo, 1980

In the beginning, it's always a seed

The first seed planted in a garden

The first seed buried in a crack in the sidewalk

The first seed of an idea

And that seed, if the elements are right, is destined to grow

How wild, how high, how fast, how fruitful is all yet to be determined

But one thing is for sure: it will grow into something

A story to unfold.

Contents

# Beginnings

*My earliest memories* are not of me in the kitchen nor around a family dining table. This often surprises people since I run a culinary business and pretty much live for cooking and entertaining. Instead, my first memories are of running barefoot in my grandparents' garden in Zimbabwe, climbing avocado and mango trees, and playing hide-and-seek with my sister, Talia. Through the thick woody bases of the banana trees, we would watch our mother and grandmother together in the garden, focused on their daily practice: planting and tending to seeds.

Growing up, I didn't know seeds would become my destiny. I did what many good daughters do and followed the straight line from university to law school to corporate lawyer. I was lucky to live and work in some of the biggest cities around the world, from Sydney (where I was born) to New York (my current home), with several years in between spent in London, Hong Kong, and Tel Aviv. I was constantly moving, making friends, eating delicious food, discovering new ingredients, and embracing countless new food cultures.

All the while, my mother's garden back in Australia grew, consistently and patiently, lusher and wilder. Each time I returned to her home, she would proudly take me through the different species of plants, trees, vines, native birds, beehives, arrays of fragrant flowers, fruits, and vegetables of all kinds. So many varieties, so much color—all of it originating from simple seeds.

When I eventually landed permanently (maybe) in the US in 2014, I knew it was time to plant some new seeds of my own, moving into an industry that felt more creatively fulfilling than corporate law. And so began my entrepreneurial journey of establishing a small food business in New York City's legendary food hall, Chelsea Market, with two cofounders, Lisa Mendelson and Monica Molenaar. Specializing in tahini, a creamy condiment made of sesame seeds, and halva, its confectionary cousin, we were the country's first shop dedicated to food made from sesame. We called it Seed + Mill, and it was a dream come true.

I've proudly watched Seed + Mill grow, with our products now sold in nearly two thousand retailers and restaurants across the country. A thriving business with products all born from one seed, that blossomed into so much more for me: a sense of purpose, a community, and a foretelling realized.

—*Rachel*

*"Do you think New Yorkers are going to know what tahini is?" . . . "Will they want to try it?" . . . "Are we crazy for wanting to start a business in such a niche food category?"*

These were just a few of the anxious questions Lisa, Monica, and I asked ourselves back in 2015 as we attempted to build a business from an idea. We launched Seed + Mill with the goal of bringing tahini and halva onto the main stage, spotlighting its taste, nutrition, and versatility. Celebrating its uniqueness, yet also making it approachable. You can still see "Tuh-hee-nee"— the phonetic pronunciation of *tahini*—displayed in large black lettering on the white tiles in our Chelsea Market stall. I love watching newcomers read those words and come over to the counter with questions.

Time and time again, I've seen the power of food to connect—to broker conversations, transcend differences, and build meaningful relationships through a shared, yet silent, love language. I live that experience almost every day at Seed + Mill, exchanging stories with tourists who might have discovered our store while wandering through New York, or with locals who have made a pilgrimage for food that reminds them of their homes, their ancestors, or their travels. I like to believe that everyone who finds themselves at our counter feels a sense of belonging, a connection to their past or perhaps their future. One of my favorite stories is of Allie and Kabir, who met for their first date over tahini soft serve at our store, and returned years later to purchase a halva cake for their wedding.

We've received so many emails from customers wanting to share their memories or personal attachment to halva or tahini that I eventually created an email folder called "Seed + Mill Pen-Pals." I've kept in touch with many of these pals for years. Indeed, the very day this manuscript was due, I received a note from Joshua, the self-declared head of the Secret Society of Halva Lovers, telling us that when he ate our halva "his heart swooned, his eyes aflutter, flooding his mind with cherished memories of traveling abroad."

Seed + Mill has afforded me the opportunity to fulfill what I cherish most in this world: a love of feeding people and my craving for human connection, and this book, by extension, is my love letter to the seed that started it all.

When I first contemplated writing this book, I was nervous about two things: Could I really create 80+ unique recipes that all included sesame? And, who was I to do it?

Answering the first of these questions was easier than the second. Over the years I have spent traveling the world, I have been introduced to an immense variety of culinary ideas. This has not only made for an exciting and delicious life, but it has allowed me to traverse vast geographic regions and food traditions and tie seemingly disparate people and places together. To my surprise, the recipe ideas came quickly and easily. Even after writing this book, I must say, I am still constantly surprised by the breadth of sesame's uses. But, at the same time, I am just one person with one viewpoint. So, when writing this book, it felt appropriate to turn to a trusted group of fellow home cooks and professional chefs from different countries and cultures for inspiration and recipe contributions.

As for who am I to be writing such a book? What cultural or geographic expertise or connection do I have to sesame? Why am I so invested in this one tiny seed?

Well, one answer is that I see myself as a lifelong student and traveler, and I am fascinated by sesame's storied history, as it moved from place to place, establishing roots in so many global culinary traditions. Another, perhaps more complex answer, is that I subconsciously recognize much of my own family's peripatetic history and feel drawn to sesame's story of migration, survival, and adaptation.

To put those feelings into context, centuries ago, my Jewish ancestors were expelled from their homes during the Spanish Inquisition and found refuge in Eastern Europe. My great grandparents lived in an area known as Bohemia and my grandparents were born in Czechoslovakia (as it was then known). After surviving the Holocaust, my grandparents found each other in Prague and left with nothing to start a new life in Bulawayo, Zimbabwe, of all places. It is here where my mother was born. But, she too did not remain in her birth country and moved to London, where she met my Australian father, who was working abroad. Together, they moved back to Sydney, where I was born and raised. I'm now living with my husband and children in New York, and truthfully, I have no idea what city or country might be next for us.

My family's predilection for moving and reinventing ourselves (even if, at times, our relocations were imposed upon us) leaves me wondering where my own culinary roots are anchored. Do I have a food culture I can call my own? In searching for answers, I've come to realize that just like sesame has moved from place to place and does not have a singular cultural identity, nor do I.

I feel so lucky to have found tremendous joy in life through travel, meeting new people, learning, adapting, and embracing a wide range of flavors and techniques in my own cooking. With a passport so full of stamps, I'm often asked, "Where feels most like home?" My simple answer: in a kitchen.

*Matthew (pictured above) was the first team member we hired at Seed + Mill and is affectionately known as the Mayor of Chelsea Market.*

My Love Letter to Sesame

# One Seed, Served Three Ways

*My objective in writing this book is to give you a broad selection of delicious recipes that use sesame as a key ingredient through the lens of all three of its most common applications:*

### Seeds

Whole black and white sesame seeds can be used to flavor a dish, add a textural crunch, or serve as a finishing seasoning, usually blended with salt and other spices. In most cases, black and white sesame seeds can be used interchangeably, although black sesame seeds tend to have a slightly bitter, nuttier flavor and contain slightly less oil. I almost always toast white sesame seeds, whereas black sesame seeds don't depend on the same caramelization process to enhance their flavor.

### Sesame oil

Sesame oil is made by pressing the whole sesame seeds rather than grinding them. The oil has a distinctly strong flavor, so it is used mainly to add flavor and body to a dish rather than for frying. White sesame seeds are used for the majority of the world's sesame oil production, but I do sometimes see black sesame oil and use it occasionally, when I'm looking for a stronger flavor.

### Tahini (sesame) paste or sesame butter

Tahini is made from grinding sesame seeds and emulsifying the oil in the center of the seed with the fibrous hull. It is an essential ingredient base for many dips and spreads, the most famous being hummus.

1. **You have more time than you think:** Tahini can last up to three years. Of course, we don't put that on our jars at Seed + Mill because we hope you'll use it faster than that. But, in reality, the main downside to "older tahini" is that eventually the fiber from the seeds will sink and the oil will rise to the top. Usually, you can give the jar a vigorous shake or stir it all back together to get it to its original consistency.

2. **Use every last drop:** Sometimes there is about an inch of seed fiber at the bottom of tahini containers that feels impossible to stir back into the paste. Don't be too quick to throw it away! My friend Hanna shared the genius idea of adding about two inches of pickle juice (or a similar acidic liquid like olive brine) before screwing the lid back on tightly and giving the jar a vigorous shake. Add some extra lemon juice, salt, and pepper, and you will have a thick, creamy dip without using a single piece of kitchen equipment.

3. **Storage matters:** Heat and light are not good for tahini or sesame oil, so I tend to store them in the refrigerator or a cool pantry. The cooler the storage temperature, the slower the separation of oil from seed fiber. When it comes to halva, we are proud of the fact that the halva we make at Seed + Mill is free of palm oil, which is an ingredient commonly used to stop oil separation and make the halva appear less greasy. So, when buying palm oil–free halva, keep it in the refrigerator to minimize the risk of oil separation.

4. **Toasting leads to big flavor:** All references to sesame seeds or sesame oil in this book refer to lightly toasted white sesame seeds or lightly toasted sesame oil (unless otherwise specified). To lightly toast white sesame seeds, place them in a skillet over medium heat, gently shaking the seeds until they are golden and fragrant, about five minutes. They burn quickly, so don't walk away!

Sesame plants are perennial and can grow up to three feet tall in hot, dry conditions.

Their bell-shaped flowers bloom in late summer and can be white, blue, or purple.

Each flower produces a pod containing up to a hundred seeds. When ripe, the pods burst open and spill the seeds to the ground, a process some believe to be the origin of the phrase "open sesame."

Each pod will burst open at a different time, so farmers typically cut the sesame stalks and allow them to ripen in a standing position, making it easier to capture the seeds.

# Sesame
## A Brief History

To add flavor, the seeds are roasted in a hot oven before being ground.

To measure the power of the sesame seed, we'd have to travel back some 5,500 years to the Indian subcontinent, where it was grown as one of the first known oilseed crops. We see sesame depicted in art and poetry and included in recipes from Ancient Greece and the Roman Empire. Archeologists have uncovered Egyptian tombs decorated with hieroglyphic illustrations of sesame seeds scattered over bread (perhaps an ancient precursor to the American hamburger bun, Jerusalem bagel, Turkish simit, Montreal bagel, or Chinese shao bing).

Over centuries, the humble sesame seed has traveled through many lands and thrived within many culinary cultures because of its delicious nutty taste, nutritional density, and long shelf life. The high levels of antioxidants in sesame allowed it to cross great distances without refrigeration and without turning rancid as quickly as other vegetable oils or animal fats. As sesame migrated around the world, local populations embraced it as their own, infusing their own traditional cooking techniques and flavors, each time expanding this small seed's possibilities.

Once ground, the seeds produce a liquid-gold paste, also known as tahini.

# The Origins of Tahini

The name tahini comes from the Arabic word *tahana*, meaning "to grind." There are several common pronunciations or ways to spell tahini, including tehina, tahina, and tahin.

Historically, the sesame seeds were soaked in salty water, roasted, and then stone ground, emulsifying their fibrous outer husk and oil in the center to create a thick, luscious paste. Not much has changed, except that the stones have been largely replaced with powerful colloid mills.

Sesame is a rich source of calcium, iron, magnesium, healthy fats, and anti-inflammatory properties, which is why tahini is often referred to as "liquid gold," loved equally for its flavor and its powerful health benefits.

Similar to the way we evaluate other prized ingredients such as chocolate, wine, or coffee, different brands of tahini will vary according to a range of factors, starting most importantly with the source of the seeds being used and their agricultural environment, or terroir. Other differentiating factors typically include:

- a seed's fiber to oil ratio
- a sweet or bitter taste profile
- the amount of salt used in the soaking liquid
- the amount of husk retained in the final product (if you see "whole seed" tahini, it means that more of the nutritious husk has been incorporated into the paste)

- roasting temperature and caramelization: is it a dark or light roast?
- whether the seeds have been single or double ground
- when the seeds were harvested, processed, and ground (given the long shelf life at each step, this will influence freshness and eventual oil separation)

# A Final Thought Before You Begin

*I love eating at restaurants* (especially in a great city like New York where there is so much diversity), but nothing comes close to the gratitude and love I feel for a friend who takes the time to cook for me or the delight I take in feeding others. As someone known for going completely over the top when preparing a dinner party, I will (sheepishly) admit that all that time worrying about whether my food or the table setting is perfect is wasted energy. No one ever comes *only* for the food and very few of us remember exactly what we ate. But, we do tend to remember how we *feel* in someone's home; an interesting conversation, a laugh, connecting with a new friend.

I found it surprisingly hard to write many of these recipes. At home, I'm not a recipe (or rule!) follower and instead cook by instinct and with lots of practice. The kitchen has always been my place of meditation and therapy—it's where I'm most comfortable taking risks and making mistakes. So, when it came to documenting each step and measuring each ingredient to develop the recipes in this book, I found it hard. Thankfully, I was able to recruit a number of patient recipe testers who have helped me craft dishes that look and taste great.

But, in the spirit of learning to enjoy cooking more at home, I would also encourage you to use this book as a gateway into the world of possibility—as inspiration for menu planning, for new or unexpected flavor combinations, or for easy and elegant plating and presentation ideas. With few exceptions, it's hard to go wrong with these recipes. All you really need is the freshest ingredients you can find, an open mind to tasting things as you go, adjusting as needed, and (hopefully) enjoying the process.

# STARTING AFRESH

# Dreamy, Creamy Banana & Sesame Smoothie

———

*Serves 1 to 2*
*Time: 3 minutes*

1 overripe banana, cut into chunks and frozen (see Note)

1½ cups unsweetened almond milk or another milk of your choice

3 tablespoons tahini

3 dates, pitted and coarsely chopped

½ teaspoon pure vanilla extract

½ teaspoon kosher salt

1 to 2 ice cubes (optional)

1 tablespoon cocoa nibs, for garnish (optional)

½ teaspoon ground cinnamon (optional)

I've seen recipes for this style of smoothie around a lot—and I hesitated to include it here as I didn't think it felt original anymore. But, it made the cut for a couple of reasons: 1. I wanted more of you to give it a try, if you haven't already, and 2. when I saw my husband spooning copious amounts of tahini into his smoothies in the morning to make his nondairy drink feel rich and creamy, it was a reminder that the versatility and awareness of tahini as a nutrition boost had come a long way.

In a food processor or blender, combine the banana, almond milk, tahini, dates, vanilla, salt, and ice cubes and process until smooth and creamy, about 1 minute. Garnish with the cocoa nibs and/or cinnamon, if desired. Serve immediately.

———

Note: *I always keep a stash of overripe bananas in a resealable bag in my freezer for spontaneous smoothies or banana bread. You can make this smoothie with a fresh, rather than frozen, banana—just consider adding extra ice to achieve a cold, creamy texture.*

Don't be deterred by the dark, moody colors of this smoothie. It might look like an ominous thundercloud, but it will leave you feeling energized and like you're starting your day on a sunny, tropical island. You can use any type of milk for this recipe, but I think the nutty complexity of the black tahini lends itself particularly well to the sweetness of the coconut milk.

In a food processor or blender, combine the banana, coconut milk, blueberries, black tahini, vanilla, ice cubes (if using), and salt, and process until smooth and creamy, about 1 minute. Taste and add the honey, if desired, and blend again until incorporated, about 1 minute. Serve immediately.

# Black Tahini, Blueberry & Coconut Smoothie

—

*Serves 1 to 2*
*Time: 3 minutes*

1 small overripe banana, cut into chunks and frozen

1 cup coconut milk or another milk of your choice

½ cup frozen blueberries

1½ tablespoons black tahini (see Note)

½ teaspoon pure vanilla extract

1 to 2 ice cubes (optional)

¼ teaspoon kosher salt

1 teaspoon honey or maple syrup (optional)

—

**Note:** *Black tahini is available on Amazon and at most specialty grocery stores.*

# Fully Loaded Granola

—

*Makes about 8 cups*
*Time: 30 minutes*

2½ cups old-fashioned rolled oats

¾ cup unsweetened coconut flakes

½ cup pecans, coarsely chopped

½ cup walnuts, coarsely chopped

½ cup pumpkin seeds

¼ cup sunflower seeds (optional)

1 teaspoon kosher salt

1 teaspoon ground cardamom

½ teaspoon ground cinnamon

½ cup maple syrup

⅓ cup extra-virgin olive oil

¼ cup tahini

3 tablespoons espresso or strong black coffee (optional; see Note)

1 teaspoon pure vanilla extract

—

**Note:** *While the coffee is what makes this recipe so unique, if you don't love its flavor, feel free to leave it out—the granola will still taste delicious.*

This recipe started as a tahini granola. I generally make a big batch once a month and thought my recipe was pretty delicious as originally written. But, a chance conversation with my friend Jimmy on the day we were due to photograph this recipe changed everything. As we were preparing the ingredients for the photo, I casually asked Jimmy what his "can't leave out" granola ingredient was. His reply was so intriguing that I gave it a try, then immediately tweaked my recipe. Jimmy's secret ingredient is . . . a shot of espresso! It makes so much sense, given many of us are usually sipping coffee while eating granola in the morning. Plus, you're left with delicious, coffee-infused milk to slurp up in your bowl once all the granola is gone.

1   Preheat the oven to 375°F and line two rimmed baking sheets with parchment paper.

2   In a large bowl, combine the oats, shredded coconut, pecans, walnuts, pumpkin seeds, sunflower seeds (if using), salt, cardamom, and cinnamon. In a medium bowl, whisk together the maple syrup, olive oil, tahini, coffee (if using), and vanilla, then pour over the oat mixture and stir until evenly combined.

3   Spread the mixture evenly on the prepared baking sheets. Bake for 15 minutes, shake the baking sheets, and lower the temperature to 325°F. Bake until golden brown, 10 to 15 minutes, vigorously shaking the baking sheets two more times and checking to make sure the mixture is not burning at the edges.

4   Cool the granola completely before serving. The granola can be stored in an airtight container at room temperature for up to 2 months.

This is a "no recipe" recipe, perfect for lazy weekend breakfasts. It's a simple, luscious combination of flavors and textures. It's a comforting dish to me because the sourdough bread has a distinctly Australian feel about it (Aussies love to eat sourdough!), but the toppings are very Middle Eastern, fusing together so many of my travel memories.

Toast the bread or leave it fresh, depending on your preference. Spread the labneh on the bread, then drizzle with the tahini and honey and finish with the flaky salt and Sweet Dukkah (if using). Serve immediately.

# An Indulgent Middle Eastern Breakfast Toast

—

*Serves 1*
*Time: 2 minutes*

1 thick slice sourdough bread

1 tablespoon labneh

1 to 2 tablespoons tahini

1 tablespoon honey or date syrup

⅛ teaspoon flaky salt

A shake of Sweet Dukkah (page 56; optional)

# Three-Seed Porridge with Caramelized Banana

——

*Serves 2*

*Time: 10 minutes, plus 30 minutes to soak (optional)*

1¼ cups old-fashioned rolled oats

2 cups whole milk or another milk of your choice

1 cup water, plus more as needed

2 tablespoons sunflower seeds

2 tablespoons white chia seeds

1 teaspoon pure vanilla extract

¼ teaspoon kosher salt

1 tablespoon unsalted butter

1 teaspoon light brown sugar, plus more as needed

1 banana, peeled and sliced lengthwise

½ teaspoon ground cinnamon

2 tablespoons tahini

1 teaspoon sesame seeds

I've been eating porridge for breakfast for as long as I can remember. For me, it is the ultimate comfort food. I started every single day of high school with a bowl of steaming porridge, topped with a generous sprinkle of Milo (an Australian chocolate malt powder loved by kids and adults alike). When I moved to New York, I learned that Americans refer to porridge as oatmeal, which I never thought sounded quite as delicious!

1   In a small, heavy saucepan, combine the oats, milk, and water. If you have the time, soak the oats for up to 30 minutes before warming them (this will give them a creamier texture).

2   Bring the mixture to a boil over medium-high heat, then turn the heat down to low and add the seeds, vanilla, and salt. Stir with a wooden spoon every 1 to 2 minutes to make sure the oats don't stick to the bottom of the pan, cooking until the liquid has been absorbed and the oats are creamy, 5 to 7 minutes.

3   While the oats are cooking, melt the butter in a medium nonstick skillet over medium heat. When the butter starts to bubble, add the sugar to the skillet and immediately place the bananas cut-side down over the sugar. Cook until nicely caramelized but not burnt on both sides, 1 to 2 minutes on each side. Don't stir the bananas, as they will become mushy— just watch them to make sure they don't burn and give the entire pan a slight swirl to move the caramelized sugar around. Remove the bananas from the heat and set aside until ready to use.

4   Before removing the oats from the saucepan, check that the texture is smooth and creamy. If it looks lumpy or too sticky, add 1 to 2 tablespoons of hot water and stir to loosen. If desired, stir in another teaspoon of brown sugar.

5   Divide the oats between two bowls and top with the bananas, cinnamon, a drizzle of the tahini, sesame seeds, and any remaining cooking liquid from the pan where the bananas were caramelized. Serve immediately. Leftover porridge can be stored in an airtight container in the refrigerator for up to 2 days. Reheat in the microwave.

# Pear & Pistachio Breakfast Loaf with Sesame Streusel

—

*Makes one 9 by 5-inch loaf*
*Time: 20 minutes,*
*plus 1½ hours to bake*

**For the streusel topping**

¼ cup all-purpose flour

1 tablespoon light brown sugar, plus 1 teaspoon

1 tablespoon unsalted cold butter, diced, plus more for greasing

⅛ teaspoon kosher salt

2 tablespoons pistachios, finely chopped

**For the cake**

1½ cups all-purpose flour

1¾ teaspoons baking powder

1 teaspoon ground cardamom

1 teaspoon kosher salt

¼ teaspoon baking soda

⅔ cup granulated sugar

⅓ cup light brown sugar

2 eggs, at room temperature

1 teaspoon pure vanilla extract

½ cup extra-virgin olive oil

½ cup tahini

1 teaspoon sesame oil

½ cup full-fat Greek yogurt

3 small pears, thinly sliced

This breakfast loaf has a dense, almost creamy, texture. It also has a savoriness that makes it less of a "cake" and more of a morning or weekend brunch treat. I think it's best enjoyed with a swoosh of butter and a hot drink. It would also make a lovely dessert, served warm with a scoop of ice cream and berries.

1  Preheat the oven to 325°F. Line a 9 by 5-inch loaf pan with parchment paper, leaving an overhang of paper on each of the long sides. Grease the parchment paper with butter.

2  **Make the streusel:** In a food processor, combine the flour, brown sugar, butter, and salt and pulse until just incorporated. Add the pistachios and pulse again until just combined. You can also prepare the streusel in a small bowl, using your fingers to combine the ingredients until the mixture resembles wet sand. Set aside.

3  **Make the cake:** In a medium bowl, whisk the flour, baking powder, cardamom, salt, and baking soda. Set aside.

4  In a stand mixer fitted with the paddle attachment or with a handheld mixer, beat the sugars, eggs, and vanilla on medium speed until the mixture is pale and fluffy, about 3 minutes. Reduce the speed to low and gradually add the olive oil, tahini, and sesame oil. Once incorporated, slowly mix in half of the dry ingredients, then half of the yogurt, scraping down the sides often, and alternating between the two mixtures, until everything is well combined. The batter will be thick.

5  Pour the batter into the prepared loaf pan. Fan out the pear slices on top of the batter, allowing them to sink slightly. Sprinkle the streusel in the gaps, making sure it goes all the way to the sides.

6  Bake until a skewer inserted in the middle comes out clean, 60 to 80 minutes. If desired, brown the top of the loaf by broiling for an additional 2 to 3 minutes. Cool for 10 minutes in the pan on a wire rack, then use the parchment flaps to lift the loaf out of the pan and cool further. Serve warm or at room temperature. The loaf can be stored in an airtight container at room temperature for up to 3 days.

Like it is for me, the food industry is a second career for Sylvie Charles. After spending ten years working as a pediatric doctor and watching her dad's struggles with diabetes, Sylvie was drawn to the health and taste benefits of dates and built a business, Just Date, with a mission of introducing more date-based sweeteners into people's meals. As an immigrant to the United States from India, Sylvie also brought her passion for the healing properties of Ayurvedic principles to her cooking. Sylvie juggles running her business with parenting her two gorgeous girls, Nava and Aya, and I have turned to her countless times in moments of crisis for hugs and moral support.

When developing this recipe, Sylvie wanted to re-create the traditional cinnamon bun experience, but replace all of the sugar with a lower glycemic sweetener option by using dates. This version is delicious and has a soft, pillowy challah dough center that you will love ripping apart.

1  **Make the dough:** Place the yeast in a large bowl. Pour ¼ cup of the date syrup over the yeast, then add 1 cup of the water. Do not stir. Let the mixture sit in a warm place until the yeast blooms and becomes foamy, 5 to 7 minutes.

2  Add the following ingredients to the yeast mixture in this order, mixing well after each addition: 1 cup of the flour, the eggs, the remaining 2 tablespoons date syrup, the salt, and ½ cup of the olive oil.

3  Add the remaining 3¼ cups flour in ½-cup increments, mixing well with a wooden spoon after each addition. When the dough starts to come together, knead with your hands until it's no longer sticky but not too dry, 3 to 4 minutes.

4  Lightly coat a large bowl with a thin layer of olive oil and place the ball of dough inside. Cover the bowl tightly with plastic wrap and let rise in a warm place for 2 hours (or let the dough rise in the refrigerator overnight).

# Pull-Apart Date & Tahini Rolls

—

*Recipe shared by*
**Sylvie Charles, MD**

*Makes 16 to 20 rolls*
*Time: 1 hour,*
*plus 2 hours to rise*

**For the dough**

1 packet (2¼ teaspoons) active dry yeast

¼ cup date syrup, plus 2 tablespoons

1 cup lukewarm (100° to 108°F) water, plus 1 teaspoon for the egg wash

4¼ cups sifted all-purpose flour, plus more as needed

2 eggs, at room temperature

1½ teaspoons kosher salt

½ cup extra-virgin olive oil, plus more for the bowl

1 egg yolk

*Continued*

## Pull-Apart Date & Tahini Rolls

—

*continued*

**For the filling**

12 large dates, pitted

½ cup date syrup

2 teaspoons date sugar (see Note)

1 teaspoon ground cinnamon

Nonstick cooking spray

**For the icing**

⅔ cup milk, plus more if needed

½ cup tahini

⅓ cup date sugar

Date syrup, for drizzling

——

*Note: Date sugar is available for purchase on enjoyjustdate.com and at some specialty grocery stores. If you can't find it, substitute 1 extra date for the sugar in the filling and ⅓ cup date syrup for the sugar in the icing.*

5  **Make the filling:** In a medium bowl, cover the dates completely with hot water and let soak for 20 minutes. Drain the dates, discarding the liquid. In a blender or food processor, blend the dates with the date syrup, date sugar, and cinnamon. Set aside.

6  Grease two 9-inch round baking pans or skillets with nonstick cooking spray.

7  Turn the dough out onto a lightly floured surface and divide in half. Working with one half at a time, roll out the dough into a 12 by 9-inch rectangle about ¼ inch thick.

8  Spread half of the filling onto the rolled-out dough, leaving a ½-inch border around the edges. Roll the dough into a tight log, starting from the short side of the rectangle. Slice the log into 8 to 10 even pinwheels, about 1¼ inches thick. Place the rolls onto the prepared pans, leaving an inch of space between rolls.

9  When ready to bake, preheat the oven to 325°F.

10  In a small bowl, prepare the egg wash by whisking together the egg yolk and the remaining 1 teaspoon water, then use a pastry brush to brush the egg wash on all sides of the rolls (you can prepare the rolls with the egg wash the night before by keeping them covered with plastic wrap in the refrigerator, then bringing them to room temperature when ready to bake).

11  Bake the rolls until they are puffy and golden brown, about 25 minutes. Set the pan on a wire rack to cool while you make the icing.

12  **Make the icing:** In a medium bowl, whisk the milk, tahini, and date syrup. Depending on the consistency of the tahini you're using, you may need to add more milk to thin out the icing. The goal is to reach a drizzly, easily spreadable consistency.

13  Spread the icing over the warm rolls in the pan and drizzle with the date syrup for a last little flourish. Leftover rolls can be stored for up to 2 days and are best enjoyed slightly reheated.

# Sweet & Salty Sesame Challah

—

*Makes 1 large round loaf or 2 small rounds*

*Time: 45 minutes, plus 3 hours to proof, plus 35 minutes to bake*

**For the dough**

1 cup warm (about 115°F) water

1 tablespoon sugar, plus ½ cup

1 packet (2¼ teaspoons) active dry yeast

1 tablespoon honey

3 eggs, at room temperature

5 to 6 cups bread flour

½ cup plus ½ teaspoon extra-virgin olive oil

2 teaspoons kosher salt

**For the challah glaze**

1 egg, at room temperature

1 teaspoon honey

1 teaspoon water

⅓ cup Gomasio (page 57), or ⅓ cup black and white sesame seeds and 1½ teaspoons flaky salt

Eating challah on the Friday night Sabbath is a treasured ritual and family tradition. If there is one recipe in this book that most defines the intersection of my cultural and culinary identity, it would be this one. Making challah feels personal. It feels meditative. And it's a tradition I hope my children will share with the next generation. I particularly love the symbolism of making a round, sweet challah on Rosh Hashanah, the Jewish New Year. The round shape represents the infinite cycle of life, offering a moment for reflection and redemption as one year ends and a new one begins. I always eat challah on the day it is baked, preferably while still warm from the oven! But, I also enjoy having a few slices left over to make French toast for Saturday breakfast.

1 **Make the dough:** In the bowl of a stand mixer fitted with the whisk attachment, combine the water and 1 tablespoon of the sugar and whisk until the sugar is dissolved. Sprinkle the yeast over the mixture and let sit until you see the mixture starting to bubble and foam, 5 to 10 minutes.

2 Add the remaining ½ cup sugar, honey, eggs, and 1 cup of the flour to the yeast mixture. Whisk on low speed until just combined, then add ½ cup olive oil and whisk again until the mixture resembles thick pancake batter.

3 Switch to the dough hook and with the mixer on low speed, gradually add the salt and 3½ cups of the remaining flour in three additions. At this stage, assess whether your dough looks shaggy (this will depend on the humidity of your workspace). In order to bring the dough together into a smooth elastic ball, add more flour, 2 tablespoons at a time, using a spatula to scrape down the sides of the bowl after each addition. When the dough starts to have a smooth and slightly elastic texture, stop adding flour and knead, with the stand mixer on medium speed, for 10 to 12 minutes, or transfer the dough to a floured surface and knead by hand—I'll do this whenever I have the time because I find the process relaxing and meditative.

4 Coat a large bowl with ½ teaspoon of the olive oil and place the dough in the bowl, turning it once so that it's oiled on all sides. Cover the bowl with plastic wrap and place in a warm spot

in your kitchen. Allow the dough to rise for at least 2 hours, or longer if you have the time. The dough should double in size.

5   When ready to braid, line one 11-inch round baking pan with parchment paper. If you are making two smaller round challahs, you will need two 8-inch round baking pans. Or you can use this dough to make any other braided shape of your choice.

6   **Make the glaze:** In a small bowl, whisk together the egg, honey, and water and set aside.

7   **Braid the dough:** Using your fist, punch the dough down in the bowl to reduce any air bubbles and then place the dough on a lightly floured work surface. Divide the dough into four equal balls and roll each ball into an 8-inch log (rounder in the

*Continued*

Starting Afresh

center and slightly tapered at the ends). Place the gomasio on a plate and roll two of the logs in it until coated on all sides.

8  Begin creating a four-strand braid by arranging two of the logs horizontally and the other two vertically, overlapping them in a weave pattern. (I recommend watching a four-strand round challah braiding video on YouTube for assistance, see Notes.)

9  Braid the dough by tucking one log under its neighbor to the left, going clockwise, then switching to go counterclockwise and tucking each log under its neighbor to the right until the ends of the logs meet. Tuck the ends under the base of the braid and place it in the prepared baking pan.

10  Brush the glaze all over the non-seeded portions of the challah, including the sides, but try not to let the glaze pool in the creases of the braids. Keep the remaining glaze for a second coat before baking. Cover it with plastic wrap and place the baking pan in a warm, draft-free spot to rise for a second time, 40 to 50 minutes, or until the dough holds the indent of your finger when lightly pressed. You can also leave the dough in the refrigerator overnight, but bring it to room temperature before baking.

11  When ready to bake, preheat the oven to 350°F.

12  Glaze the non-seeded portions of the challah a second time. Bake until the bread is golden brown, about 35 minutes. You can also test the challah for doneness by tapping it and listening for a hollow sound.

———

Notes: *I use a stand mixer to make challah, but it is also perfectly doable to make it by hand if you have the time and energy for kneading! Sometimes, I start with the mixer and finish the kneading by hand.*

*I haven't included detailed instructions for braiding the dough, as there are so many variations on how to do this. This recipe has been created for one large or two small round challahs, using a four-strand braiding technique. I learned how to braid challah by watching other people do it at home, in baking classes, and through countless instructional YouTube videos. For this recipe, I highly recommend searching for a four-braid round challah video online and watching before you start braiding.*

There are pretty defined family roles in our kitchen. I am more than a bit bossy and I usually insist on playing head chef. One of my kids is sometimes willing to play sous chef. And my gracious husband, Chris, cleans up the hurricane that's invariably left behind. But, there are a few recipes that have exceptions to these rules, and this is one of them. Unless Chris gets to play head chef for soft scrambled eggs, my kids won't eat them. His technique and seasoning are perfect and had to be shared in this book!

1   In a small bowl, whisk the eggs, milk, and a pinch or two each of salt and pepper until well combined, 1 to 2 minutes.

2   In a large skillet, melt the butter over medium heat, allowing the butter to start bubbling and fully coat the bottom of the skillet. Be careful not to let it burn. Pour in the egg mixture and let it sit in the skillet for 15 seconds without stirring.

3   Using a heatproof spatula or wooden spoon, very gently move the egg mixture around the pan from one side to the other. Do not stir or whisk the egg mixture once it's in the skillet. As you sweep the eggs from side to side, tilt the pan toward the heat so that the mixture pools on one side at a time, about 2 minutes total. The gentle sweeping and tipping movement will help the eggs cook at a consistent temperature and eventually create fluffy clouds of eggs. Watch the heat setting carefully so that the eggs don't brown.

4   When ready to serve, sprinkle the eggs with the Gomasio and scallion and drizzle with the sesame oil. Serve immediately with the warm tortillas or toast, and finish with the avocado or any other favorite breakfast side.

# Soft Scrambled Eggs with Gomasio

—

*Serves 2*
*Time: 10 minutes*

4 eggs

½ cup whole milk or heavy cream

Kosher salt and freshly ground pepper

1 tablespoon unsalted butter

1 tablespoon Gomasio (page 57)

1 scallion, green and white parts thinly sliced on the diagonal

1 teaspoon sesame oil

Warm tortillas or toasted bread

Sliced avocado (optional)

# Halva at Home

—

*Recipe shared by*
Kristina Costa

*Makes 12 squares*
*Time: 10 minutes,*
*plus 1 hour to set*

2¼ cups (500g) tahini,
at room temperature

¾ teaspoon kosher salt

2 cups plus 3 tablespoons
(420g) sugar

1 cup water

2 tablespoons Sweet
Dukkah (page 56) or
toasted sesame seeds
(optional)

My friend Ivy is one of those people who always knows the best places to eat. Her suggestions are not necessarily fancy or listed in a city guide. Ivy is just an avid traveler, always on the hunt for places with a story. So, when she took me to Loquat, a bakery in San Francisco, I didn't doubt that we were in for a treat.

I sat down, ordered coffee, and was immediately taken by the beautiful design of the store, especially the elegantly restored counter, reminiscent of an old European cafe. When my drink arrived, I was surprised and delighted to find a small cube of halva sitting on the saucer—a sweet accompaniment to the coffee! The halva was perfectly made—not too sweet and with a soft, delicate texture. Knowing the challenges of creating good halva, I was impressed and asked if I could meet the pastry chef. A few minutes later, Kristina Costa emerged from the kitchen and joined us for a chat about all things sesame and the Middle Eastern influence of her pastry program. If you visit San Francisco, you must add Loquat to your itinerary. But, in the meantime, Kristina has generously shared Loquat's halva recipe so you can make it at home.

1  Line a 12 by 8-inch baking pan with parchment paper.

2  In a large bowl, combine the tahini and salt.

3  In a medium saucepan, combine the sugar and water, stirring with a spoon until it's the texture of wet sand. Cook the sugar mixture over medium heat until a candy thermometer consistently reads 250°F, 8 to 10 minutes.

4  Slowly pour the sugar mixture into the bowl with the tahini and gently fold together with a wooden spoon until the mixture is well combined and forms a loose dough. Be careful not to overmix or the halva will end up crumbly.

5  While the dough is still warm and malleable, spread it onto the prepared baking pan so that it reaches about 1½ inches up the side of the pan.

*Continued*

Halva at Home

—

*continued*

6 Sprinkle the dough with the Sweet Dukkah or the sesame seeds, if desired.

7 Allow the halva to set in the pan until cooled completely, about 1 hour, then store in the fridge until ready to serve.

8 When ready to serve, tip the halva out of the pan and slice it into squares. Homemade halva can be stored in an airtight container in the refrigerator for up to 6 weeks.

—

Note: *For best results, I recommend using a kitchen scale rather than measuring by cups here.*

Sesame

# A Brief History of Halva

*"Halva is like a delicate, precious stone, carved from the quarries of history."*

SHARED BY A SEED + MILL CUSTOMER, 2016

The word halva translates to "sweet" in Arabic and its history stretches back hundreds, if not thousands, of years. First appearing in the Middle East, it quickly spread through major trade routes to Eastern Europe, India, and South America.

Originally made with dates and milk, this sweet, fudge-like confection eventually became more commonly made with crushed sesame seeds, which is the way we make it at Seed + Mill. But, it can be made with a variety of other seeds, grains, and nuts, such as semolina, pepitas, sunflower seeds, and peanuts.

Historically, it was such a cherished sweet that Suleiman the Magnificent, famous sultan of the Ottoman Empire, was believed to have built a separate kitchen just for halva, known as the "Helvahane" or "House of Halva." A recipe for making halva was included in one of the first known cookbooks, *Kitab al-Tabikh*, or *"The Book of Dishes,"* written in the thirteenth century.

Rumi, the thirteenth-century Afghan poet and philosopher, references halva in one of his famous romantic poems, "This Marriage," still often recited today at weddings: "May these vows and this marriage be blessed. / May it be sweet milk, / this marriage, like wine and halvah." As a romantic and history enthusiast, our store manager and very first employee at Seed + Mill, Matthew, likes to keep a copy of Rumi's poetry in the top drawer at our counter, just in case he can persuade a lingering customer to engage in conversation about the history of our products.

What distinguishes halva most from other desserts or confections is its unique texture and flavor: flaky but not crumbly, dense but not chewy, sweet but not cloying. What a marvelous alchemy! It should literally melt in your mouth. Over the years at Chelsea Market, we've learned that the best way to describe its virtues is just to encourage people to taste it for themselves. So we share hundreds of samples with visitors every day, watching people's reactions to its unusual and ancient qualities.

# Spiced Tahini Hot Chocolate

—

*Makes 2 cups*
*Time: 10 minutes*

2 cups oat milk, or another milk of your choice

½ teaspoon ground cinnamon

¼ teaspoon ground cardamom

4 ounces 70% dark chocolate, coarsely chopped

3 tablespoons tahini

½ teaspoon pure vanilla extract

⅛ teaspoon kosher salt

Honey (optional)

The addition of tahini to a classic hot chocolate gives the drink an earthy flavor and a boost of extra creaminess. It's hard to describe the difference in words, but once you've tried it, you will know what I mean! It's so good, I've now started adding a tablespoon of tahini to matcha and chai as well.

1  In a small saucepan, combine the milk, cinnamon, and cardamom and cook on medium to high heat until hot but not boiling, 3 to 4 minutes. Turn the heat down to low and add the chocolate, tahini, vanilla, and salt and stir with a spoon until the chocolate has melted.

2  Remove the saucepan from the heat and use a whisk or small milk frother to beat the mixture until the ingredients are well combined and starting to froth.

3  Taste and add 1 to 2 teaspoons honey, if desired, for sweetness. Stir well and serve immediately.

# SESAME
# SEASONINGS
# & SAUCES

# Dukkah

I first tasted dukkah, a crunchy, fragrant spice blend made with a combination of nuts, seeds, and spices, as an eighteen-year-old backpacker traveling through Egypt. During high school and while at college, I focused a lot of my studies on ancient Egyptian history and have visited Egypt many times, traveling from top to bottom. One of my strongest food memories is sitting on a rickety wooden stool in an alleyway in Cairo, devouring warm flatbread drizzled with olive oil and coated in dukkah. Dukkah is very easy to make at home, and I love having a jar in my pantry to use for finishing off a salad, scrambled eggs, or avocado toast. The sweet version is nice sprinkled over poached fruit, yogurt, and toast with labneh and honey and can also be used as a cookie dough topper.

## Savory Dukkah

*Makes about 1½ cups*
*Time: 10 minutes*

½ cup pistachios, coarsely chopped

½ cup almonds, coarsely chopped

½ cup sesame seeds

1 teaspoon toasted coriander seeds, crushed

½ teaspoon cumin seeds

½ teaspoon fennel seeds (optional)

1½ tablespoons flaky salt

1 tablespoon coarsely ground pepper

1  Start by toasting the pistachios and almonds in a small skillet over medium heat for 2 to 3 minutes, carefully watching to make sure they don't burn. Add the sesame seeds, coriander, cumin, and fennel, if desired, to the skillet. Cook for another minute, stirring frequently to make sure the seeds don't burn, then remove from the heat.

2  Working in small batches, place the mixture in a mortar and pestle (see Note) and lightly pound. I like to have a variety of textures in my dukkah, so I often crush some of the batches more than others. Combine everything in a large bowl and mix in the salt and pepper, adding more if needed. Transfer to a tightly sealed container. Dukkah will last up to 2 months in the pantry or up to 4 months in the freezer.

———

Note: *Dukkah is not usually made with almonds, but I happen to like the texture and taste they add to this blend (you can always substitute them with hazelnuts). I usually crush my nuts and seeds in a mortar and pestle for a rustic texture, but you can also use a food processor for a finer blend.*

*Continued*

Sesame

## Sweet Dukkah

*Makes about 2½ cups*
*Time: 15 minutes*

1 cup sesame seeds

½ cup pistachios, coarsely chopped

½ cup almonds, coarsely chopped

½ teaspoon ground cinnamon

½ teaspoon ground cardamom

½ teaspoon flaky salt

½ cup unsweetened coconut flakes

2 tablespoons edible dried rose petals (optional, see Note)

___

**Note:** *Edible dried rose petals are available online and at many specialty grocery stores.*

1   Preheat the oven to 375°F. Line a rimmed baking sheet with parchment paper.

2   Spread the sesame seeds, pistachios, and almonds on the prepared baking sheet. Sprinkle with the cinnamon, cardamom, and salt and toss to evenly combine.

3   Bake for 6 minutes, then give the baking sheet a vigorous shake to move the nuts and seeds around. Add the coconut to the mixture and shake the baking sheet again. Return the mixture to the oven and bake until the coconut has turned golden brown, 4 to 6 minutes more. Check regularly to make sure the dukkah isn't burning.

4   Cool the dukkah completely on the pan before adding the rose petals (if using). Store in an airtight container in the pantry for up to 2 months.

# SESAME SEASONINGS

## Furikake

*Makes about ⅓ cup • Time: 10 minutes*

¼ cup well-toasted white sesame seeds
(see page 17)

2 tablespoons black sesame seeds

2 to 3 large sheets roasted nori, cut into
thin strips with kitchen shears

1 teaspoon flaky salt

¼ teaspoon sugar

½ teaspoon red chile flakes (optional)

½ teaspoon shiitake mushroom powder
(optional)

In a mortar, combine the seeds, nori, salt, and
sugar. Add the chile flakes and mushroom
powder (if using). Use a pestle to lightly grind
and break down the sesame seeds, releasing
some of their oils. Taste and add more salt,
sugar, or chile flakes as desired. Transfer the
mixture to an airtight container and store at
room temperature for up to 3 months.

## Gomasio

*Makes 1 cup • Time: 10 minutes*

1 cup well-toasted sesame seeds (see page 17)

¼ cup flaky salt

In a mortar, combine the sesame seeds and
3 tablespoons of the salt, using a pestle to
grind them into a coarse meal. Alternatively,
combine the seeds and salt in a food processor
and blitz until you are happy with the texture.
Stir in the remaining 1 tablespoon salt. Store
the gomasio in an airtight container at room
temperature for up to 1 month or freeze for
up to 4 months.

## Sumac Sesame Salt

*Makes ½ cup • Time: 10 minutes*

3 tablespoons well-toasted sesame seeds
(see page 17)

3 tablespoons ground sumac

2 teaspoons flaky salt

1 teaspoon red chile flakes or Aleppo pepper

½ teaspoon edible dried rose petals
(optional; see Note, page 56)

In a mortar, use a pestle to pound the sesame
seeds until coarsely ground, or leave them
whole if you prefer a crunchier texture.
Transfer the seeds to a medium bowl and add
the sumac, salt, chile flakes, and rose petals (if
using). Stir to combine. Transfer the mixture
to an airtight container and store at room
temperature for up to 2 months.

## Everything Bagel Seasoning

*Makes about ⅓ cup • Time: 10 minutes*

4 teaspoons toasted white sesame seeds
(see page 17)

3 teaspoons black sesame seeds

2 teaspoons poppy seeds

2 teaspoons granulated garlic

2 teaspoons onion flakes

1 teaspoon flaky salt

In a small bowl, combine the seeds, garlic,
onion flakes, and salt. Transfer the mixture
to an airtight container and store at room
temperature for up to 3 months.

## Sumac Sesame Salt

This blend comes from my friend Hanna, who always keeps a jar handy, ready to spontaneously sprinkle over a plate of labneh, crusty bread, or roasted vegetables! The sumac gives the salt a lovely crimson color and adds a slightly fruity, tangy flavor.

—

Note: *Sumac is a tart, red spice used in Middle Eastern cooking. Its name comes from "summaq," an Arabic word that translates to "deep red." Available at most grocery stores or online, sumac is made by grinding the dried berries from the Rhus coriaria shrub.*

## Furikake

Furikake is so popular in Japan that you see it on tables almost as often as you see salt and pepper. The word "furikake" translates to "the act of sprinkling over," and I like it over a bowl of steamed or fried rice or homemade popcorn.

## Gomasio

Gomasio is a Japanese seasoning that literally translates to sesame ("goma") and salt ("sio"). Used extensively in both restaurants and homes as an all-purpose style condiment, it adds a salty, umami flavor to any dish.

## Everything Bagel Seasoning

This book felt naked without including Everything Bagel Seasoning, a beloved, sesame-forward blend. I sprinkle it liberally on everything from salads to scrambled eggs.

# Lessons in Tahini Chemistry

I've included several of my favorite tahini sauces and tahini-based dips in this book. Each of them works as a delicious salad dressing and can also be drizzled generously over grilled proteins, bread, roasted vegetables, or crudités.

The most simple tahini sauce is typically made by combining equal parts tahini with a liquid (either water or lemon juice or a mixture of both) and a hefty pinch of salt. I like to think of this as the "mother sauce" of the Middle East. From here, anything is possible with the addition of spices, herbs, alliums, pastes, vinegars, and oils.

The most fundamental tip I want to share when making a tahini sauce is that adding the liquid to the sesame paste will feel incredibly counterintuitive. At first, the liquid will cause the tahini to seize, forming a thick, clumpy, gluey paste rather than the creamy sauce you might have hoped for. Do not panic! As someone who has probably made more tahini sauce in a week than most will make in a lifetime, I can assure you that it will always get to the consistency you want with a bit of patience. After a minute of whisking the liquid with the tahini, you should eventually achieve a slightly paler (if using white sesame tahini), creamy consistency, ready to flavor with seasoning, garlic, herbs, etc. If your sauce is too thin, add a bit more tahini. If it's too thick, add more water, lemon juice, or vinegar to thin it out. Always taste before serving and adjust your seasoning to your preference.

## Walnut Tahini Tarator

*Makes about 1½ cups • Time: 10 minutes*

¾ cup toasted walnuts, slightly cooled
¾ cup water, or more as needed
½ cup tahini
2 tablespoons extra-virgin olive oil
Juice of 1 lemon
1 garlic clove
1 teaspoon kosher salt
½ teaspoon freshly ground pepper

1   In a food processor, blitz the walnuts to a fine meal (a little bit of texture is also fine if you prefer your sauce chunky).

2   Add the water, tahini, olive oil, lemon juice, garlic, salt, and pepper to the food processor and pulse until your desired consistency is achieved, adding more water, a little at a time, if necessary, to loosen.

—

**Note:** *Each of these dressings or sauces will last up to 5 days in the refrigerator. Give each a good stir or shake before using.*

## Vegan Tahini Caesar Dressing

*Makes ½ cup • Time: 5 minutes*

¼ cup tahini
Juice of 1 lemon
2 teaspoons capers, minced
1 teaspoon Dijon mustard
1 garlic clove, minced
2 tablespoons water, or as needed
Kosher salt and freshly ground pepper

In a small bowl, whisk the tahini, lemon juice, capers, mustard, and garlic until well combined. Add 2 tablespoons of the water, season with the salt and pepper, and whisk until thick and creamy. Add more water, a little at a time, to achieve your desired consistency.

## Tahini Miso Sauce

*Makes 1 cup • Time: 5 minutes*

⅓ cup tahini
Juice of 1 lemon
¼ cup extra-virgin olive oil
2 tablespoons white miso
1 tablespoon maple syrup
1 garlic clove, minced
Kosher salt and freshly ground pepper
2 tablespoons water, or more as needed

In a small bowl or in a blender, combine the tahini, lemon juice, olive oil, miso, maple syrup, and garlic, and season with the salt and pepper. Whisk or blend until smooth and creamy. Mix in the water. If needed, add more water, a little at a time, to achieve your desired consistency.

# Sunny Sauce

*Makes about 1 cup • Time: 5 minutes*

½ cup tahini

1½ teaspoons ground turmeric,
plus more for color

Juice of 1 lemon

1 teaspoon date syrup or maple syrup

1 teaspoon kosher salt

1 garlic clove, minced

Freshly ground black pepper

In a small bowl, combine the tahini,
1½ teaspoons of the turmeric, the lemon juice,
date syrup, salt, and garlic and whisk until
thick and creamy. Season with the pepper
and add more turmeric for color, if desired.

# Spicy Green Tahini Sauce

*Makes about 1½ cups • Time: 10 minutes*

4 garlic cloves, unpeeled

1 large jalapeño

2 tablespoons extra-virgin olive oil

½ bunch cilantro

½ bunch flat-leaf parsley

1 cup fresh dill

½ cup water

½ cup fresh lime juice (about 2 limes)

¾ cup tahini

¾ teaspoon kosher salt

Freshly ground pepper

1  Preheat the oven to 400°F.

2  Place the garlic and jalapeño on a rimmed
baking sheet and toss with the olive oil. Roast
until browned, about 15 minutes. Set aside.

3  Coarsely chop the cilantro, parsley, and
dill and add to a high-speed blender with
½ cup water and the lime juice. Blend until
it becomes a smooth, bright green paste.
Add the tahini and salt and season with the
pepper. Blend until fully incorporated, about
1 minute.

4  Cut the roasted jalapeño in half, scrape
out and discard the seeds, and set the halves
aside to cool. Squeeze the garlic from the
skins.

5  Add the jalapeño and garlic to the blender
and blend until smooth and creamy.

Each of these dressings shines as an accompaniment or dipping sauce to many recipes in this book. They can all be substituted for one another, depending on your preference for texture and color, as well as what's in your pantry. Good quality tahini is the only nonnegotiable ingredient!

Walnut Tahini Tarator,
page 62

Tahini Miso Sauce,
page 62

Vegan Tahini Caesar Dressing,
page 62

Sunny Sauce,
page 63

Spicy Green Tahini Sauce,
page 63

# DIPS, CRACKERS & SNACKS

# Not Another Hummus Recipe

—

*Serves 4 to 6*
*Time: 20 minutes*

1 pound dried chickpeas, or 1 (15-ounce) can chickpeas

1 tablespoon baking soda

3 garlic cloves, minced

Juice of 2 lemons

1 teaspoon kosher salt, plus more as needed

Freshly ground pepper

2 cups tahini, plus more as needed

1 to 2 tablespoons ice water, as needed

Extra-virgin olive oil, for drizzling

——

**Note:** *If you are entertaining, you can make hummus up to 3 days in advance and store it in an airtight container in the fridge. Bring to room temperature before serving. Hummus will form a skin after an hour or so, so I recommend reblending the hummus in the food processor just before serving or giving it a vigorous stir by hand.*

I debated whether to include this recipe. There's no shortage of easily accessible hummus recipes. Indeed, out of curiosity, I asked ChatGPT how many hummus recipes exist in the world and was told: "It's difficult to provide an exact number, as new recipes are continually created. Thousands of hummus recipes are available online, showcasing the versatility of this popular dish." But, given the starring role tahini plays as an ingredient when making hummus, it felt almost scandalous to leave this recipe out. No other dish has done more than hummus to get tahini into people's pantries.

Once you realize how easy it is to make at home—and how much better it tastes—I promise you'll reconsider ever buying hummus from the grocery store again!

1  If using dried chickpeas, soak them overnight or for up to 48 hours in a large bowl with enough water to cover. Drain the chickpeas, then place them in a medium saucepan and cover with water. Add the baking soda and cook over medium heat until the chickpeas are soft, about 30 minutes. Drain, reserving ½ cup of the cooking liquid. Peeling the chickpeas is optional—personally, I don't have the patience and don't mind the slightly chunkier texture the skins leave. If using canned chickpeas, reserve 2 tablespoons of the liquid from the can, then drain the chickpeas.

2  In a food processor, combine the cooked or canned chickpeas, garlic, and the 1 to 2 tablespoons reserved cooking or canned liquid and process on high speed for 1 minute. Add the lemon juice and 1 teaspoon salt and season with pepper. Process until smooth, about 2 minutes more.

3  Add the tahini and blend until the hummus has a creamy, pillowy texture, 2 to 3 minutes. If the hummus feels too thick or chunky, add the ice water and blend for 1 minute more. If the hummus feels too thin, add 1 to 2 more tablespoons tahini and blend until you are happy with the texture.

4  Taste and add more salt and pepper if needed. Serve with a drizzle of olive oil and more freshly ground pepper.

# Winter Hummus Plate

—

*Serves 2 to 4*
*Time: 30 minutes*

3 tablespoons extra-virgin olive oil, plus more for drizzling

2 tablespoons maple syrup or honey

½ teaspoon ground cumin

½ teaspoon kosher salt

½ large kabocha squash, sliced into 1- to 2-inch-thick wedges, skin and seeds retained (see Note)

2 cups Not Another Hummus Recipe (page 68) or store-bought hummus

½ teaspoon flaky salt

Freshly ground pepper

Pita or crusty bread, for serving

I usually dread the end of the warmer months, but there are certainly a few silver linings, including the arrival of all the interesting squash varietals. For this dish, I used kabocha squash because I love the way it roasts. It will virtually melt on the inside and form a deliciously sweet, caramelized edge. It is not traditional to serve hummus with squash wedges on top, but I like the combination of flavors and how the roasted squash is enhanced by the creamy base.

1  Preheat the oven to 400°F. Line a rimmed baking sheet with parchment paper.

2  In a small bowl, whisk the olive oil, maple syrup, cumin, and kosher salt. Coat the squash wedges in the marinade and arrange them on the prepared baking sheet, allowing space between each wedge so they crisp rather than steam in the oven.

3  Roast for 15 minutes, then turn over the wedges. Roast until the squash is caramelized on the outside and soft in the center, another 15 minutes.

4  Swoosh the hummus on a plate or large bowl, then pile the wedges on top.

5  Top with flaky salt, pepper, and a drizzle of olive oil and serve with the pita or crusty bread.

—

Note: *I very rarely throw out the seeds when roasting squash as they are delicious and, in my opinion, only add more flavor, texture, and nutrition to your plate.*

Every summer I try to plant a couple of cherry tomato vines. The very simple joy of watching a tomato vine grow and flower, and then finally plucking the tomatoes off one by one as they're ready to eat, is truly one of life's greatest pleasures.

1  Preheat the oven to 275°F.

2  Place the tomatoes and garlic cut-side down in a 13 by 9-inch baking dish then drizzle with the olive oil and season with the salt and pepper.

3  Roast the tomatoes and garlic until the tomato skins are starting to burst, 50 to 55 minutes. Allow the tomatoes to cool slightly (or completely).

4  Swoosh the hummus on a plate or large bowl, then pile the tomatoes and garlic on top (you can squeeze the softened garlic from the skins or leave the whole head on the plate as more of a garnish). Top with the dukkah and a drizzle of olive oil and serve with the pita or crusty bread. Serve immediately. The hummus, roasted tomatoes, and garlic can be made up to 3 days in advance of serving and kept in an airtight container in the refrigerator.

# Summer Hummus with Garlic-Roasted Cherry Tomatoes

—

*Serves 2 to 4*
*Time: 1 hour*

1 pound cherry tomatoes, in a mixture of shapes, colors, and sizes, vines and stems left on

1 unpeeled garlic head, halved horizontally

¼ cup extra-virgin olive oil, plus more for drizzling

½ teaspoon flaky salt

Freshly ground pepper

2 cups Not Another Hummus Recipe (page 68) or store-bought hummus

1 teaspoon Savory Dukkah (page 54)

Pita or crusty bread, for serving

Winter Hummus Plate,
page 70

Not Another Hummus Recipe,
page 68

Summer Hummus with
Garlic-Roasted Cherry
Tomatoes, page 71

This is a relatively fuss-free recipe that works well as a dip for crackers, a crudité board, or as a delicious base for grilled proteins in a more substantial meal. Last year, I made it for the Jewish New Year because it reminded me of tzimmes, a sweetened carrot dish traditionally served during the Rosh Hashanah meal. Ironically, the colloquial meaning of the Yiddish word tzimmes is "to make a big fuss," which this recipe is not. Perhaps it was harder to peel the carrots and open your spice drawer back in the 1800s!

1  In a medium saucepan, combine the carrots with enough water to cover and bring to a simmer over medium heat. Reduce the heat to low, cover, and cook for 10 minutes.

2  Remove the lid and continue cooking until all of the water has evaporated.

3  Add the olive oil to the saucepan, increase the heat to medium, and allow the carrots to brown on all sides, tossing occasionally to ensure they don't burn, about 5 minutes. If you'd like, set aside a few of the cooked carrots to use later as a garnish.

4  Transfer the carrots to the bowl of a food processor. Add the tahini, honey, salt, sumac, cumin, red chile flakes, paprika, garlic, and lemon juice and pulse until smooth(-ish). I prefer this dip on the chunkier side, but you can also keep pulsing until it's completely smooth. If the dip feels too chunky after blending, add 1 to 2 tablespoons water to thin it out.

5  To serve, smooth out the dip on a large plate and use the back of a spoon or spatula to create a shallow well in the center or around the edge of the plate. Fill the well with extra tahini, the sesame seeds (if using), pepper, and the reserved cooked carrots (if using). Serve immediately or store in an airtight container in the refrigerator for up to 3 days.

# Caramelized Carrot Dip

—

*Makes about 2 cups*
*Time: 25 minutes*

4 large carrots, peeled and chopped into ½-inch pieces

¼ cup extra-virgin olive oil

¼ cup tahini, plus more for drizzling

1 tablespoon honey

½ teaspoon kosher salt

¼ teaspoon ground sumac

¼ teaspoon ground cumin

¼ teaspoon red chile flakes

¼ teaspoon smoked paprika

2 garlic cloves

Juice of 1 lemon

1 teaspoon sesame seeds (optional)

Freshly ground pepper

# Golden Roasted Potatoes with Muhammara

---

Serves 3 to 4
Time: 25 minutes plus 1 hour
for the potatoes

1½ pounds baby yellow potatoes or fingerling potatoes, halved

1 tablespoon plus 1 teaspoon kosher salt, plus more as needed

5 to 7 tablespoons extra-virgin olive oil, plus more for drizzling

4 large red bell peppers

½ cup plus 1 tablespoon toasted walnuts, coarsely chopped

⅓ cup panko bread crumbs

2 tablespoons tahini

1 tablespoon pomegranate syrup

Juice of ½ lemon

1 teaspoon smoked paprika

1 teaspoon Aleppo pepper or other red chile flakes

Freshly ground black pepper

Muhammara is a traditional Syrian dip made primarily from roasted red peppers and walnuts. It doesn't usually call for tahini, but after some experimenting, I found the tahini to be a worthy addition. I usually serve this dish with pita or a grilled piece of chicken or fish, but for this recipe, we're enjoying it alongside a simple bowl of golden roasted potatoes.

1  Preheat the oven to 400°F.

2  In a large saucepan, combine the potatoes with enough water to cover and 1 tablespoon of the salt, then bring to a boil over high heat. Cook until the potatoes are only slightly tender when pierced with a knife, 15 to 20 minutes. Drain and return the potatoes to the saucepan on the stove without heat for a minute to allow all of the water to evaporate.

3  Place the potatoes on a sheet pan, and toss with 3 to 4 tablespoons of the olive oil and the remaining 1 teaspoon salt. Roast until golden brown, 50 to 60 minutes, giving the sheet pan a vigorous shake midway through.

4  Meanwhile, prepare the bell peppers. Place the peppers directly onto the flame of a gas burner at the highest heat. You can also place the peppers on a grill pan or outdoor grill. Allow the skins to blister and blacken, turning as needed. Remove the peppers from the heat once the skins have charred, about 15 minutes per pepper.

5  Transfer the peppers to a resealable plastic bag, then seal it to steam the peppers for about 10 minutes (this step will make it far easier to remove the skins).

6  Remove the peppers from the bag then rub the skins off, remove the stems, and scrape out the seeds.

7  In a food processor, combine the peppers, ½ cup of the walnuts, panko, the remaining 2 to 3 tablespoons olive oil, tahini, pomegranate syrup, lemon juice, paprika, and Aleppo pepper and blend until you're happy with the consistency. Taste and season with black pepper and more salt, if necessary.

8  Serve with the dip on the side or swoosh the dip onto a plate, top with the potatoes, and garnish with the remaining 1 tablespoon walnuts. The dip and potatoes can both be stored in an airtight container in the refrigerator for up to 3 days.

"Who else has a crush on Chef Ayesha?" I asked the crowd at the legendary De Gustibus Cooking School inside Manhattan's Herald Square Macy's. Every single hand went up. It was around 2018 and I had met Ayesha a few months earlier at her new Middle Eastern-inspired restaurant Shuka in the Soho neighborhood of New York City, where a similar version of this dip is always on the menu. Ayesha had kindly invited me to share the De Gustibus stage with her to talk about the history of tahini for a few minutes. Ayesha's energy, warmth, and sense of humor are so infectious that you can't help but want to be in her orbit. Not long after her successful launch of Shuka, Ayesha opened its sister venue, Shukette, which has since won several accolades for spectacular food and warm hospitality. Born to an Indonesian dad and Italian mom, Ayesha brings a versatile and unique approach to her food, clearly savoring a sense of adventure and fun with her restaurants. I always feel like a member of the extended Shukette family when I visit, and I couldn't be more thrilled that Ayesha agreed to share this recipe in my book.

# Pistachio and Whipped Feta

—

*Recipe shared by*
*Ayesha Nurdjaja*

*Serves 4 to 6*
*Time: 20 minutes*

1 cup raw pistachios

2 tablespoons tahini

½ teaspoon kosher salt, plus more as needed

1 garlic clove

½ cup crumbled feta

1 bunch cilantro, leaves only

Zest and juice of ½ lemon

2 tablespoons extra-virgin olive oil, plus more for drizzling

Freshly ground pepper

Pita bread or grilled protein, for serving

1   In a food processor, pulse the pistachios until finely chopped, about a minute. Add the tahini, salt, and garlic and pulse until evenly combined.

2   Add the feta and cilantro. Pulse a few times to bring the mixture together. With the food processor running, slowly stream in the lemon juice and olive oil to emulsify. If the dip is sticking to the sides of the food processor, add 1 to 2 tablespoons water and pulse again to thin out. Fold in the lemon zest and season with pepper and more salt to taste.

3   Serve with the pita bread or the grilled protein. The dip can be stored in an airtight container in the refrigerator for up to 5 days.

# Deconstructed Baba Ghanoush

—

*Recipe shared by*
Lior Lev Sercarz

*Serves 4 to 6*
*Time: 25 minutes*

3 to 4 eggplant

Juice of 2 lemons

¼ cup extra-virgin olive oil

2 garlic cloves, minced

1 to 2 teaspoons smoked sea salt (available online or at specialty grocers)

½ cup tahini

½ red onion, thinly sliced

½ cup chopped cilantro

1 to 2 teaspoons Urfa chile, depending on your heat preference

Pita or bread, for serving

—

**Note:** *Always serve with fresh pita or bread to soak up the juices.*

Lior's beloved spice shop, La Boîte, is next door to my kids' school in Manhattan. He opened La Boîte in 2006, after a decade of working in some of the best professional kitchens in France and New York. When we launched Seed + Mill, I stopped into Lior's shop to see if he would be open to creating a range of globally inspired, sesame-forward spice blends for us that represented the food cultures of the Middle East (Za'atar), Japan (Togarashi), and New York (Everything Bagel).

Over the subsequent years, Lior has become a mentor and dear friend—a dream guest who arrives with a cooler (named Elvis . . . doesn't everyone name their cooler?!), which is always full of unique food gifts, produce, spices, and, if you're extra lucky, a bottle of the most heavenly olive oil from his father Moishe's olive grove in Israel. The eggplant flesh literally melts into a soft pillowy canvas, just begging to absorb all of the flavor from the tahini, lemon, and spices.

1  The eggplant can be charred in a few different ways: Place them directly on a gas burner over medium-high heat until the skin has blackened, turning the eggplant every 2 to 3 minutes. You can also broil it on a baking sheet in your oven or directly on an outdoor grill, turning every 2 to 3 minutes, for about 15 minutes total. The eggplant is ready when the flesh is soft and the skin has a wrinkled and blackened char all over. Set aside to cool.

2  In a small bowl, whisk the lemon juice, olive oil, garlic, and salt until combined. Set aside.

3  Place the eggplant on a serving plate and slice down the center, leaving the stem intact (for aesthetic purposes only!).

4  Gently open up each eggplant and use a fork to flatten and spread out the eggplant flesh to cover the plate. Drizzle the tahini and lemon juice mixture over the eggplant.

5  Finish by sprinkling with the onion, cilantro, and Urfa chile and serve with pita. The egglant can sit at room temperature for a few hours before serving. If you are planning to make this a day ahead, refrigerate the peeled eggplant in a covered container and bring to room temperature before serving. Drizzle with the tahini.

Sesame

Mona and her partner, Kate, are the creators of Talbott & Arding, a beloved provisions shop in upstate New York. Mona was the first to ask if we would wholesale our tahini. While I was thrilled at the prospect of seeing our products out in the wild, I had no idea what starting a new sales channel involved. Mona and Kate patiently supported us through months of finding our feet—there were lost deliveries, exploded tahini buckets, and out of stock challenges. I try to visit Talbott & Arding at least a couple of times a year to see what's new and chat with their knowledgeable team. The last time I was there, I discovered (or perhaps more accurately, inhaled) this sesame focaccia.

1  In a large bowl, combine the flour, salt, and yeast and whisk to incorporate. Add the water and stir until a shaggy dough forms.

2  With one hand holding the bowl steady and the other on the dough, fold the dough onto itself from the bottom center to the top center. Do this five or six times, turning the bowl counterclockwise as you flip the dough. Loosely cover the bowl with plastic wrap and let the dough rise for 2 hours at room temperature.

3  Once the dough has risen, divide ¼ cup of the olive oil between two 9-inch round baking pans. Cut the dough in half and place each half into one of the oiled pans. Lightly stretch the dough to even it out and fill the pan.

4  Cover the pans loosely with plastic wrap and transfer to the refrigerator for 6 to 8 hours. The dough will slowly cold proof and develop a more complex flavor.

5  Lift the dough to unstick from the bottom of the pans, then gently stretch and pat it back to the edges of the pans. Return it to the refrigerator to proof again, covered with plastic wrap, until the dough has risen and doubled in size, about 1 hour.

6  Preheat the oven to 450°F. Using your fingertips, dimple the dough evenly, creating deep indentations. Drizzle with the remaining ¼ cup olive oil and sprinkle the sesame seeds over the top.

7  Bake until the crust is bubbly and golden brown, 13 to 17 minutes. Let cool in the pans for 10 minutes before serving. Focaccia is best eaten the day it is baked.

# Sesame Focaccia

—

*Recipe shared by*
**Mona Talbott**

*Makes two 9-inch round loaves*

*Time: 47 minutes, plus 8 to 9 hours to rise and proof*

525g all-purpose flour

1 tablespoon kosher salt

1 teaspoon instant yeast

2 cups warm (110 to 115°F) water, plus 1 tablespoon

½ cup extra-virgin olive oil

2½ tablespoons raw sesame seeds

# Seeded Nori Crackers

—

*Makes about 20 crackers*
*Time: 1 hour*

1 cup chia seeds

½ cup thinly sliced scallions

¼ cup lightly toasted sunflower seeds

¼ cup pumpkin seeds

¼ cup white sesame seeds

3 tablespoons nori flakes, crushed or coarsely chopped

1 teaspoon garlic powder

1 teaspoon red chile flakes

1½ teaspoons kosher salt

1 cup boiling water

1 teaspoon flaky salt

These crackers are easy to make and are terrific as a tasty, gluten-free snack. I usually purchase all of the seeds in bulk, as they last a long time and I like to have them on hand for other recipes like Fully Loaded Granola (page 28), Three-Seed Porridge with Caramelized Banana (page 32), and the Sweet Seed & Nut Snack Bites (page 87).

1  In a large heat-safe bowl, combine all of the ingredients except for the water and flaky salt and stir to evenly incorporate.

2  Add the water to the seed mixture and stir again to combine. Cover the bowl with plastic wrap or a kitchen towel and let sit for 10 to 15 minutes at room temperature to allow the chia seeds to absorb most of the water.

3  While the seeds are sitting, preheat the oven to 350°F (using the convection setting if possible) and line two rimmed baking sheets with parchment paper.

4  Once the water has been mostly absorbed, divide the seed mixture between the two prepared sheets and spread it evenly over the parchment paper until it's about ¼ inch thick, using a spatula to smooth it out. To achieve an even, very thin layer, place another piece of parchment paper over the mixture and use a rolling pin to smooth it out until it reaches the edges of the baking sheets.

5  Remove the top layer of parchment paper (if using). Bake the seed mixture until it looks firm and slightly golden, 40 to 45 minutes.

6  Remove from the oven. If you would like the crackers to be thinner, place a piece of parchment paper over the mixture while still hot and use a rolling pin to roll thinner. Sprinkle with flaky salt, and let cool completely before breaking into shards.

7  Store the crackers in an airtight container at room temperature for up to 1 month.

These sweet snack bites are incredibly satisfying as an afternoon treat or for a boost of energy on a hike or long bike ride! You can use this recipe as a base and add in whatever other ingredients you have in your pantry. Sometimes I mix in hemp, chia seeds, or poppy seeds, dried cherries or apricots—essentially whatever's on hand when I spontaneously decide to whip these up. There's no right or wrong—just keep adjusting the ratio of dried seeds and nuts with the tahini and softened fruit until you are happy with the texture and flavor and the balls hold their shape.

1 Make the balls: In a medium bowl, soak the dates in boiling water until soft, about 10 minutes, then drain.

2 Place the nuts in a food processor and pulse until finely chopped. I like a bit of extra texture, but you can also blend until they resemble a coarse flour meal.

3 Add the soaked dates, the tahini, cacao nibs, and salt to the food processor with the nuts and pulse until the mixture is combined, scraping the sides of the bowl midway. The mixture should resemble a sticky dough. Taste and add a pinch more salt, if desired. I prefer not to add any additional sweetener, but if you have a sweet tooth, add in the maple syrup to your liking.

4 Scoop 10 golf ball–size portions of dough and roll them in the palm of your hand until rounded.

5 Place the desired coating in a shallow bowl and roll each ball in the coating until well covered. If the coating doesn't stick, roll the balls in a touch of date syrup or maple syrup before adding the coating.

6 Refrigerate the balls for 30 minutes, until firm, then serve.

# Sweet Seed & Nut Snack Bites

—

*Makes about 10 golf ball-size bites*

*Time: 15 minutes to prepare, plus about 30 minutes to firm up, depending on your preferred texture*

**For the balls**

10 medjool dates, pitted

1 cup toasted almonds, pecans, or hazelnuts (or a mix of any of these)

3 tablespoons tahini

2 tablespoons cacao nibs

½ teaspoon kosher salt, plus more if needed

1 to 2 tablespoons maple syrup or date syrup, plus more to taste and for rolling (optional)

**For the coating**

¼ cup coating of your choice (such as shredded coconut, cacao powder, sesame seeds, finely chopped pistachios, or beet powder)

—

Note: *These will last in an airtight container in the freezer for up to 3 months, and I especially love to eat them super cold, straight from the freezer.*

# Crunchy Sumac Chickpeas

—

*Makes 2 cups*
*Time: 20 minutes*

—

1 (15-ounce) can chickpeas, drained

2 tablespoons extra-virgin olive oil

1 tablespoon tahini

1 to 2 tablespoons Sumac Sesame Salt (page 57; see Note)

—

*Note: Any of the sesame salt seasonings from pages 57 to 59 will work for this recipe.*

When we first started Seed + Mill, Monica, Lisa, and I worked from each other's homes if we weren't at Chelsea Market, and we often made a big, shareable salad for lunch. I don't remember who came up with the idea of coating chickpeas in tahini before roasting them, but it quickly became a favorite salad topper or afternoon snack! The tahini makes a fantastic glue for the seasoning.

1  Preheat the oven to 425°F. Line a rimmed baking sheet with parchment paper.

2  Pat the chickpeas dry with a paper towel. They need to be very dry before you add the oil and seasonings or they won't crisp. If you have the time, to maximize the crispiness, I recommend placing the chickpeas on the prepared baking sheet in the fridge overnight, uncovered, before roasting.

3  In a large bowl, toss the chickpeas with the olive oil, tahini, and Sumac Sesame Salt to taste until evenly coated.

4  Spread the chickpeas on the prepared baking sheet, taking care not to crowd them together—this will help them crisp up in the oven rather than steam.

5  Bake until crispy, 15 to 20 minutes. The chickpeas can be stored in an airtight container at room temperature for up to 1 week.

Jill was one of the first "food industry" people I met not long after we opened Seed + Mill. She and her brother Rob, who was the head chef at the Food Network at the time, stopped by our store one day to chat. They had grown up eating halva and were excited to see how we were reinventing it. When we first met, Jill was in the early stages of building her now renowned blog, *Feed The Swimmers*, named after the copious amounts of food she would prepare for her ravenous teenage swimmers and their teammates. Jill is a talented and generous home cook, embracing every season with gusto and always inspiring me to get to the farmers' market, to whip up whatever dish she has shared that week.

These apricot crumble bars are "just sweet enough" and make a wonderful accompaniment to a morning or afternoon cup of tea or coffee.

1  **Make the apricot filling:** Place the apricots in a large bowl and cover with the boiling water. Allow the apricots to soak for about an hour and then remove them with a slotted spoon, reserving the soaking liquid. Cut the apricots into quarters.

2  Add the apricots, reserved soaking water, brown sugar, lemon juice, and salt to a medium saucepan, adding more water, if necessary, to fully cover the apricots. Bring to a simmer over medium heat and cook until the liquid is syrupy and reduced by half, about 20 minutes. Add the vanilla and stir, then add the cornstarch and stir until dissolved. Remove from the heat and set aside—the syrup will continue to thicken as it cools (this step may be done a day or two in advance—just refrigerate the filling in an airtight container until ready to use).

3  **Make the crust and crumble:** Preheat the oven to 335°F and put a rack in the center.

4  Generously butter an 8 by 8-inch pan. Butter one side of each of two pieces of parchment paper, and press them firmly into the pan, butter-side down and perpendicular to each other, to form a sling. This will make removing the bars much easier.

# Apricot & Halva Crumble Bars

—

*Recipe shared by*
**Jill Fergus**

*Makes 16 bars*

**For the apricot filling**

2 cups (300g) whole dried apricots

2½ cups boiling water

⅓ cup light brown sugar

Juice of ½ large lemon

½ teaspoon kosher salt

½ teaspoon pure vanilla extract

2 teaspoons cornstarch

**For the crust and crumble topping**

½ cup (113g) salted butter, at room temperature and cut into cubes, plus more for greasing

½ cup plus 3 tablespoons packed light brown sugar

¼ cup tahini

2 cups all-purpose flour

⅓ cup old-fashioned rolled oats

¼ cup sesame seeds

½ teaspoon kosher salt

¼ teaspoon ground cardamom

4 ounces halva

*Continued*

## Apricot & Halva Crumble Bars

—

*continued*

1 to 2 tablespoons
turbinado sugar

2 to 3 tablespoons
pistachios, chopped

5  In a large bowl, use a handheld mixer or sturdy fork to beat the butter and brown sugar together until smooth, then add the tahini and continue beating until the mixture is smooth.

6  In a medium bowl, whisk together the flour, oats, sesame seeds, salt, and cardamom. Stir the flour mixture into the butter mixture until fully incorporated—the dough will have a lumpy, sandy texture and not be cohesive. Press a little more than half of the dough onto the bottom of the prepared pan, creating an even and firm (but not too tightly packed) layer. The base of a measuring cup can be very helpful here to press down the dough and smooth it out. Bake the crust for 10 minutes.

7  While the crust bakes, transfer the remaining dough to a small bowl, squeeze it into loose clumps and crumbles, and place it in the freezer.

8  Remove the pan from the oven (keep the oven on) and spread the apricot filling in an even layer over the crust, staying just shy of the edges. Sprinkle the halva in an even layer over the filling, followed by the frozen crumble. Scatter the turbinado sugar over top and return the pan to the oven to bake for 30 minutes.

9  Keeping the oven on, remove the pan from the oven and sprinkle the pistachios over the top of the bars, then return the pan to the oven for about 5 minutes more, or until the topping is a deep golden brown and the filling is gently bubbling.

10  Allow the bars to cool in the pan on a wire rack for 10 minutes. Use the parchment overhang to gently lift the bars from the pan and transfer them (with the parchment paper), back onto the rack. Cool completely before slicing into bars or squares (unless you can't wait, then slightly warm is okay!). These bars will last up to a week if kept in an airtight container at room temperature.

## Sweet & Savory Grazing Boards

To me, a grazing board represents abundance, creative expression, a variety of tastes and textures, and a chance to try "a little bit of this and a little bit of that."

I love the way a grazing board placed at the center of a table allows us to linger over a lively conversation, full of laughter and a robust exchange of ideas. Or, perhaps your conversation has a quieter and more intimate atmosphere. Either way, the board will sit at the center, silently beckoning you to pause, take a breath, take a bite, and enjoy the feeling of being nourished.

The boards pictured in this book are all vintage bread boards. I love the idea that they have travelled and been passed down through families, bearing witness to countless gatherings.

The following pages feature several of the recipes in this book, including Mona's Sesame Focaccia (page 83), Ayesha's Pistachio & Whipped Feta (page 79), Mariana's Alegrías with Coconut & Anise (page 166), Golden Roasted Potatoes with Muhammara (page 76), Not Another Hummus Recipe (page 68), Seeded Nori Crackers (page 84), and chunks of Seed + Mill halva.

# CRAVEABLE SALADS & VEGETABLE SIDES

# Rainbow Carrot Goma-ae Salad

—

*Serves 6 to 8*
*Time: 10 minutes*

⅓ cup well-toasted sesame seeds

1½ tablespoons sesame oil

1 tablespoon soy sauce

1 tablespoon dashi powder (see Note)

1 tablespoon rice vinegar

1 tablespoon water

1 teaspoon mirin

1 teaspoon granulated garlic or garlic flakes

1 teaspoon kosher salt, plus more as needed

½ teaspoon honey or maple syrup

¾ pound rainbow carrots, shaved with a vegetable peeler

3 or 4 scallions, sliced on the diagonal (optional)

——

Note: *Dashi powder is available online, at Asian markets, and at many well-stocked grocery stores.*

A staple at virtually all Japanese restaurants, the classic goma-ae salad is the perfect way to start a meal or complement a main course. The term "goma" means "sesame" in Japanese and the "ae" is a reference to sauce—the mixing of vegetables with sesame dressing.

The most common way to make a goma-ae salad is to pour the dressing over wilted spinach, but any other fresh or cooked vegetables work equally well, including these lovely rainbow carrots. Shaved carrots not only look pretty on the plate, but create more surface area for the delicious dressing to cover!

1  In a mortar with a pestle or in a food processor, grind the sesame seeds until some of the oil has been released and the seeds are slightly crushed, but the mixture has not yet become a paste. Instead, it should look like crunchy wet sand.

2  In a medium bowl, whisk the ground sesame seeds, sesame oil, soy sauce, dashi powder, rice vinegar, water, mirin, granulated garlic, 1 teaspoon salt, and the honey until well combined. Taste and add more salt, if desired. Set aside.

3  In a serving bowl, toss the dressing with the carrots until evenly coated. Top the carrots with the sliced scallions (if using) and serve immediately.

The robust Tahini Caesar dressing in this salad is balanced beautifully by the bitter radicchio leaves—and I like to think that the showstopping pink leaves make for the ultimate date night salad. I like to use Castelfranco radicchio, which can be found at farmers' markets and specialty grocery stores, but Cavolo Nero or regular kale work well too. For a heartier meal, add roast chicken or an ancient grain like farro.

1   Wash and trim the core from the radicchio and pull the leaves apart. If using kale, remove the stem from the leaves and tear the leaves into large pieces.

2   In a small bowl, combine the shallots, vinegar, honey, and salt. Stir, then set aside to soften and pickle, at least 5 minutes.

3   **Make the croutons:** In a large nonstick skillet, heat the olive oil over medium-high heat. When the oil is hot, add the bread to the pan and cook until golden, about 3 minutes, then turn the pieces to cook on the other side for about 3 minutes more, making sure the bread doesn't burn. Transfer to a plate or bowl and let cool.

4   **Make the dressing:** In a food processor, combine the anchovies, lemon juice, 3 tablespoons of the water, the Pecorino, garlic, salt, and a pinch or two of pepper and process until smooth. With the machine running, slowly add the tahini until you have a thick but still pourable dressing. Taste and add more salt, pepper, water, or a teaspoon or two of the pickling liquid from the shallots, as needed.

5   To assemble, in a large bowl, toss the radicchio in the dressing and top the salad with the eggs, pickled shallots (discard unused pickling liquid), croutons, and more Pecorino.

# Radicchio Tahini Caesar

*(The Ultimate Date Night Salad)*

—

*Serves 3 to 4*
*Time: 20 minutes*

1 head Castelfranco radicchio or a large bunch of kale

2 shallots, finely sliced

2 tablespoons white wine vinegar

1 teaspoon honey

½ teaspoon kosher salt

### Croutons

2 tablespoons extra-virgin olive oil

2 to 3 thick slices of sesame-crusted sourdough, torn into 1-inch pieces

### Dressing

3 boquerones (white anchovies)

Juice of 1 large lemon

3 to 4 tablespoons water, plus more as needed

⅓ cup finely grated Pecorino, plus more for serving

1 garlic clove, minced

½ teaspoon kosher salt, plus more as needed

Freshly ground pepper

⅓ cup tahini

3 soft-boiled eggs, cut in half, for serving

# Thai-Inspired Tahini, Lime & Broccoli Salad

—

*Serves 4 to 6*
*Time: 20 minutes*

—

2 pounds broccoli, stems and leaves included (about 2 crowns)

¾ cup thinly sliced scallions (3 to 5 scallions)

½ cup tahini, plus more as needed

½ cup fresh lime juice (2 to 3 limes)

2 tablespoons soy sauce

2 teaspoons hot honey (see Note)

1 garlic clove, finely grated

1 cup chopped fresh cilantro

1 cup chopped fresh mint

½ cup lightly salted roasted peanuts, coarsely chopped

2 tablespoons sesame seeds

—

**Notes:** *If you can't find hot honey, add 1 teaspoon red chile flakes to 2 teaspoons regular honey or agave (a great vegan alternative).*

The fresh, tangy flavors of this broccoli salad were inspired by my many trips to Thailand. Traveling from Australia to Europe or the Middle East usually calls for a refueling stop somewhere in Asia. I've often used this stopover to explore the markets, islands, and jungles of Thailand. While tahini is not traditionally used in Thai cuisine, I found it gave this salad a nice creamy texture, perfectly balancing the lime's acidity.

1  Trim about 1½ inches from the ends of the broccoli stalks and peel the stalks to remove the tough outer layer. Cut off the florets, leaving as much of the stalk as possible intact. Set the florets aside. Using the shredding or julienne blade of a food processor, a mandoline, or a sharp knife, julienne the stems and place them in a large bowl.

2  Chop the florets into ½-inch pieces and add them to the bowl with the stems. Add the scallions.

3  In a small bowl, combine the tahini, lime juice, soy sauce, hot honey, and garlic and whisk until smooth. If the dressing is too thick, add 1 to 2 tablespoons of water. If the dressing seems too thin, add 1 to 2 tablespoons more tahini.

4  Pour the dressing over the vegetables and toss thoroughly to coat. Set the mixture aside to sit at room temperature for at least 15 minutes, tossing occasionally, to allow the broccoli to soften slightly. You can also cover the bowl and refrigerate the dressed broccoli for up to 8 hours before serving.

5  Just before serving, sprinkle the broccoli with the herbs, peanuts, and sesame seeds. Toss well.

One year, our Seed + Mill team held a work retreat at the end of summer, when the fresh produce is abundant and so full of flavor that you really don't want to eat anything but fruit and vegetables. While grilling some fresh corn, our head of sales, Laura, was showing us photos from her recent trip to Mexico and of the incredible corn she had enjoyed there. Elote, or Mexican street corn, is grilled corn with a creamy topping of mayo sauce, cheese, chipotle chile powder, and lime. But what if we used tahini as the creamy component? And that was how this fresh, tangy, creamy summer salad was born!

1   If using fresh corn, I love to grill it (rather than steam) to char the kernels and infuse it with smoky flavor. If you don't have a grill, you can place the corn directly on the burner of a gas stove to achieve a similar flavor, turning the cobs with tongs until lightly charred. If using canned corn, spread the kernels on a baking sheet and roast in the oven at 400°F for 5 to 6 minutes, until slightly crisp (or just skip this step altogether if you're short on time). Let the corn cool slightly.

2   While the corn is charring, in a small bowl, combine 2 tablespoons of the lime juice, shallots, and garlic and set aside to marinate slightly for 3 to 4 minutes.

3   If using cobs, once the corn has slightly cooled, use a serrated knife to slice the kernels off of the cob. Place the kernels in a large bowl.

4   When ready to serve, add the lime mixture, remaining lime juice, tahini, cilantro, jalapeño, and scallions to the bowl with the kernels and season with salt and pepper. Toss until well combined. Taste and adjust the seasoning as needed. Serve immediately. Leftovers can be stored in an airtight container in the refrigerator for up to 2 days.

# Corn Salad with a Tahini Twist

—

*Serves 4 to 6*
*Time: 20 minutes*

5 ears fresh corn, shucked, or 2 (15-ounce) cans corn kernels, drained

Juice of 2 to 3 limes

2 shallots, finely sliced or minced

1 garlic clove, minced

½ cup tahini

1 large bunch cilantro, stems and leaves finely chopped

1 jalapeño, seeded and thinly sliced

2 or 3 scallions, white and green parts finely sliced

Kosher salt and freshly ground pepper

# Japanese Cabbage Salad with Creamy Miso Sauce

—

*Serves 6*
*Time: 30 minutes*

**For the salad**

1 large Napa or green cabbage, core removed and leaves finely shredded

3 tablespoons rice vinegar

2 tablespoons sesame oil

1 tablespoon soy sauce

1 teaspoon finely grated fresh ginger

½ teaspoon light brown sugar

Kosher salt (optional)

1 bunch scallions, thinly sliced

¼ cup plus 1 teaspoon toasted almonds

3 tablespoons plus 1 teaspoon sesame seeds

**For the sauce**

½ cup tahini, plus more as needed

½ cup ice water

Juice of 1 lime

1½ tablespoons white miso

1 tablespoon soy sauce

I often make a version of this salad to accompany a protein, like grilled chicken or fish, but sometimes I find myself craving just the salad. I could eat an entire bowl for a complete meal and be well and truly satisfied.

1  **Make the salad:** Place the cabbage in a bowl of ice water for a few minutes while you make the dressing. This will crisp up the leaves.

2  In a large bowl, whisk the vinegar, sesame oil, soy sauce, ginger, and brown sugar until well combined and the sugar is dissolved. Taste and add a pinch of salt if desired (I prefer it less salty).

3  **Make the sauce:** In a small bowl, whisk the tahini, ice water, lime juice, miso, and soy sauce until it is thick and creamy. If the sauce seems too thick, add 1 tablespoon water to loosen it, or if it's too thin, stir in 1 tablespoon tahini until you have a creamy texture that is spreadable on a plate.

4  When ready to serve, drain the cabbage leaves and pat them dry. Add the cabbage, scallions, ¼ cup of the almonds, and 3 tablespoons of the sesame seeds to the bowl with the ginger-soy dressing and toss to combine.

5  Dollop the miso tahini sauce on a large plate and use the back of a spoon to spread it out toward the edge of the plate, leaving a well in the center. Place a large pile of the dressed cabbage on top, allowing a border of the sauce to remain.

6  Sprinkle the salad with the remaining 1 teaspoon almonds and 1 teaspoon sesame seeds. Serve immediately. The cabbage and dressing and can be prepared up to 3 days in advance and stored in an airtight container in the refrigerator before assembly.

Note: I prefer this salad served warm. If making a day ahead, keep the undressed salad in the fridge, and bring to room temperature before serving, adding the dressing at the last minute.

I love this kind of salad. Its mix of color and textures creates a lovely festive bowl for a gathering. But it works equally well as a clean-out-the-fridge kind of meal. Feel free to swap any of the grains, greens, or roasted vegetables with whatever you have on hand. The only nonnegotiable is the tahini, which acts as the glue holding everything together—an ingredient as ancient as the grains it is binding!

1   Preheat the oven to 400°F and line a rimmed baking sheet with parchment paper.

2   **Make the dressing:** In a small bowl, whisk the tahini, vinegar, and salt until smooth. Season with pepper and set aside until just before you are ready to serve the salad.

3   **Make the salad:** Add the squash to the baking sheet and toss with 2 to 3 tablespoons of the olive oil and season with salt and pepper. Roast the squash for 25 minutes, until tender. Transfer to a large bowl.

4   In a medium saucepan, cook the grains according to package instructions. You can prepare the squash and grains up to a day in advance and keep stored in airtight containers in the refrigerator.

5   When the grains are cooked, add the kale to the saucepan over the top of the grains, cover, and remove from the heat. Let stand until the kale is wilted, about 5 minutes. Drain any excess liquid and transfer to the bowl you used for the squash. Season with salt and pepper, then toss together with the squash. Set aside.

6   In a medium skillet, warm the remaining 2 tablespoons of the olive oil over medium-high heat. Add the shallots and a pinch of salt and cook until just starting to brown, 3 to 4 minutes, being careful not to let the shallots burn. Add the garlic and cook for 1 minute more. Add the wine and reduce the heat to low, stirring until the liquid has evaporated, about 2 minutes. Scrape the shallot and garlic mixture into the bowl with the grains and squash and toss to combine.

7   Just before serving, toss the salad with the dressing and top with the almonds and pomegranate seeds. Serve warm or at room temperature.

# A Hearty Bowl of Ancient Grains

—

*Serves 6 to 8 as a side dish or 3 or 4 as a main meal*

*Time: 40 minutes*

**For the dressing**

⅓ cup tahini

2 tablespoons red wine vinegar

½ teaspoon kosher salt

Freshly ground pepper

**For the salad**

1 small butternut squash, peeled and diced into ½-inch cubes (about 3 cups)

4 to 5 tablespoons extra-virgin olive oil

Kosher salt and freshly ground black pepper

1½ cups of your favorite ancient grain (freekeh or farro are my favorites)

10 ounces Tuscan kale, stems removed and leaves torn or sliced into strips (about 4 cups)

½ cup minced shallots (about 3 small shallots)

2 garlic cloves, minced

⅓ cup dry white wine

½ cup toasted almonds, coarsely chopped

¼ cup pomegranate seeds

# Cauliflower Salad with Sesame-Pickled Fennel

—

*Serves 2 to 4*
*Time: 40 minutes,*
*plus 1 day to pickle*

**For the pickled fennel**

1 large fennel bulb, thinly sliced, fronds reserved

2 dried bay leaves

1¼ cups white wine vinegar

1¼ cups water

1 tablespoon sugar

1 teaspoon kosher salt

1 teaspoon whole black peppercorns

½ teaspoon ground turmeric

¼ teaspoon red chile flakes

¼ cup sesame oil

**For the salad**

1 large cauliflower head, core and stems cut into 1-inch chunks

1 garlic head, halved horizontally

3 tablespoons extra-virgin olive oil

1 teaspoon kosher salt

½ teaspoon freshly ground pepper

½ teaspoon ground cumin

¼ cup toasted almonds

1 tablespoon currants, soaked for 1 minute in boiling water

1 cup labneh

This is a great salad for entertaining—it combines a unique set of ingredients that work nicely together and look pretty on a plate! Serve this salad with a grilled protein such as chicken or fish, or mix in some couscous for a vegetarian meal on its own.

1  **At least a day in advance, make the pickled fennel:** Place the sliced fennel and bay leaves in a large glass jar. In a small saucepan over medium heat, combine the vinegar, water, sugar, salt, peppercorns, turmeric, and red chile flakes, stirring until the sugar and salt have fully dissolved, 2 to 3 minutes. Pour the warm liquid over the fennel and allow the liquid to come to room temperature. Add the sesame oil to the jar, seal with a lid, shake well, and refrigerate for at least 24 hours before serving. Give the jar a shake before using.

2  **Make the salad:** Preheat the oven to 400°F. Line a rimmed baking sheet with parchment paper.

3  In a large bowl, combine the cauliflower, garlic, olive oil, salt, pepper, and cumin and toss until the cauliflower and cut side of the garlic are well coated.

4  Spread the cauliflower mixture evenly on the prepared baking sheet, arranging the garlic halves so they are cut-side down. Roast until the cauliflower and garlic are golden brown but not charred, 25 minutes, rotating the baking sheet halfway through. Set aside to cool slightly, then squeeze the garlic from its skin.

5  When ready to serve, in a large bowl, combine the cauliflower, garlic, toasted almonds, currants (discard the water), 1 cup of the pickled fennel, and the reserved fennel fronds in a large bowl. Add 1 teaspoon of the pickling liquid and toss to combine. Taste and add more salt and pepper if needed.

6  **To assemble:** Smear a plate with the labneh and top with the salad. Serve immediately with plenty of fresh bread.

—

Note: *The pickled fennel needs to be made a day prior to serving this salad. This recipe will make more pickled fennel than needed for the salad, so you will have leftovers to enjoy. Store it in the refrigerator for up to 1 month.*

# THE MAIN EUENT

# Spiced Chickpea Curry

—

*Recipe shared by*
**Nisha Vora**

*Serves 6*
*Time: 1 hour*

**For the ground spices**

1½ teaspoons curry powder

1 teaspoon ground coriander

½ teaspoon ground cinnamon

½ teaspoon freshly grated nutmeg

¼ teaspoon turmeric

Freshly ground black pepper

**For the curry**

2 tablespoons avocado oil or another neutral oil

2 teaspoons coriander seeds

1 heaping teaspoon cumin seeds

15 to 20 fresh curry leaves, or 30 dried curry leaves (optional, see Note)

1 large yellow or red onion, chopped

6 garlic cloves, minced

I stood behind Nisha in a buffet line at a dinner in Brooklyn, hosted by The Feedfeed in 2017. I didn't know anyone else in the room, but could tell Nisha was a warm, kind soul before I even introduced myself to her. She immediately made me feel at ease as we chatted about our shared history as former lawyers who had followed our passion for food into new chapters of our careers. Nisha runs a wildly popular food blog, Rainbow Plant Life, which is a beloved home for vegan recipes.

Many of Nisha's recipes are inspired by her Indian ancestry, including this dreamy chickpea curry. Although tahini isn't a traditional addition to an Indian curry, Nisha used it to create an ultra-rich, generously spiced sauce, flawlessly fusing together Middle Eastern and Indian flavors. I like to serve this curry with rice, couscous, or fresh bread.

1  **Prepare the ground spices:** In a small bowl, stir together the curry, ground coriander, cinnamon, nutmeg, turmeric, and several grinds of pepper and set aside. Fill a small bowl with a bit of water and keep it nearby for deglazing.

2  **Make the curry:** In a 12-inch heavy skillet or medium Dutch oven, warm the oil over medium-high heat. Add the coriander and cumin seeds and toast, tossing frequently until aromatic and darker by a few shades, about 1 minute (don't let them burn!).

3  Add the curry leaves, watching out for oil splatter, and cover the pan with a lid. If using fresh curry leaves, cook for just 20 seconds to prevent burning. For dry leaves, cook a few seconds longer.

4  Add the onion and a big pinch of salt and cook for 5 minutes, stirring frequently, until the onions begin to brown. If the spices start to burn, lower the heat to medium. If the onion is browning too quickly, add a splash of water.

*Continued*

Sesame

## Spiced Chickpea Curry

—

*continued*

2-inch piece fresh ginger, minced or grated

1 to 3 serrano peppers, diced (1 for mild heat, 3 for spicy!)

2 tablespoons tomato paste

½ pound Roma or plum tomatoes, diced

2 teaspoons kosher salt, plus more as needed

2 (15-ounce) cans chickpeas, drained and rinsed

1 (13.5-ounce) can full-fat coconut milk

½ cup water

3 tablespoons tahini

½ teaspoon sugar

1 small head Swiss chard or Tuscan kale, stems removed and leaves thinly sliced

2 teaspoons garam masala

1 tablespoon fresh lemon or lime juice

½ cup chopped cilantro leaves

½ cup chopped mint leaves

Rice or flatbread, for serving

5  Add the garlic, ginger, and serrano peppers and cook, stirring frequently, for 1 to 2 minutes.

6  Add the ground spices and tomato paste and cook, stirring frequently, for 90 seconds. If it gets too dry, add a splash of water.

7  Add the tomatoes and salt. Use a flat spatula to scrape up browned bits, incorporating them into the tomato juices. Cook until the tomatoes are soft and the oil starts to release from them, about 5 minutes.

8  Pour in the chickpeas, coconut milk, water, tahini, and sugar. Stir well and bring to a simmer over medium-low heat. Cover and simmer, stirring occasionally, for 15 to 20 minutes.

9  Add the Swiss chard, cover the pot, and continue simmering until the Swiss chard is tender and wilted, 4 to 5 minutes. Stir in the garam masala.

10  Remove the curry from the heat. Stir in the lemon juice and sprinkle with the cilantro and mint. Taste and season with salt. Let the curry rest for 5 to 15 minutes to allow the flavors to meld, then serve with the rice or flatbread. The curry can be stored for up to 3 days in the refrigerator and heated before serving.

—

*Note: If you have an Indian grocery store accessible to you, seek out fresh curry leaves for this recipe, which will add incredible flavor. If fresh leaves are not available, you can order dried curry leaves online.*

## A Glimpse into the History of Sesame Oil, the "King of Oils"

Sesame oil traces back thousands of years and has been used for a range of purposes, including for food, religious rituals, wellness, and beauty treatments. It became a vital trade commodity in many ancient civilizations.

From a culinary perspective, sesame oil is sometimes referred to as gingelly oil and has a strong, distinctive flavor that's been widely embraced across a number of Asian countries, including Japan, China, Korea, and India. In India, where Ayurvedic medicine has heavily influenced food and diet, sesame oil is so valued that it is frequently referred to as the "King of Oils."

Speaking of royalty, I once heard that Queen Cleopatra used sesame oil as a moisturizer and mixed it with pigments to create her distinctive eye makeup. But my favorite sesame fun fact was something our modern-day makeup queen, Bobbi Brown, once said to me about tahini: "It's like moisturizer, but for your insides."

Jamie Wei is one fascinating woman. After moving to New York from Taiwan in 2011, Jamie met her future husband on a plane—yes, for all the romantics out there, you never know where chatting to a stranger in the next seat might lead!

While Jamie's first foray into cooking focused on learning more about her new husband's Jewish culture, after her mother passed away, she found herself wanting to re-create traditional recipes from her childhood as a means to process her grief. When Jamie and I first cooked a meal together in my home, she arrived with her mother's forty-year-old rice cooker that she had brought with her to the US. We agreed that everything tastes better when prepared with an extra pinch of memory and nostalgia. Eventually, Jamie's calling to food compelled her to leave her career in fashion to start her blog, Chopsticks Meet Fork, where she shares a fusion of Taiwanese and Jewish recipes. The recipe below is a popular Taiwanese dish that transports Jamie back to the busy street markets of her hometown of Taipei.

# Spicy Sesame Noodles

辣味麻醬麵

———

*Recipe shared by*
**Jamie Wei**

*Serves 2*
*Time: 10 minutes*

1 (7-ounce) package Youmian noodles (see Note)

3 tablespoons tahini

2 tablespoons chili crisp

1 teaspoon soy sauce

1 teaspoon rice vinegar

1 teaspoon sesame oil

1 teaspoon honey

1 cup finely chopped cilantro leaves

2 tablespoons black sesame seeds

1   Prepare an ice bath in a large bowl.

2   Cook the noodles to al dente according to the package instructions. Drain, reserving ⅓ cup of the cooking water.

3   Transfer the cooked noodles to the ice bath.

4   In a medium bowl, whisk the tahini, chili crisp, soy sauce, vinegar, sesame oil, and honey until well combined. Stir in the reserved cooking water 1 tablespoon at a time until you achieve your preferred consistency—the sauce should be pourable but not watery.

5   Transfer the noodles to the sauce and mix until evenly coated. Top with the cilantro and sesame seeds and serve. The noodles can be stored in an airtight container in the refrigerator for up to 3 days.

———

Note: *Youmian noodles are commonly used in Southern Chinese cuisine and can be found online or at Asian supermarkets, but if necessary, you may substitute with lo mein or chow mein noodles.*

The Main Event

# Vegetarian Tahini Ramen

—

*Serves 4*
*Time: 45 minutes*

**For the broth**

6 cups vegetable broth

2 cups water

¼ cup soy sauce

3 tablespoons white miso

2 tablespoons rice vinegar

2 garlic cloves,
finely diced

1 tablespoon peeled,
grated fresh ginger

¼ cup tahini

Kosher salt (optional)

**For the ramen**

4 Japanese eggplant
or 1 large regular eggplant,
sliced into rounds

2 tablespoons
vegetable oil

2 pounds mixed
mushrooms (such
as enoki or shiitake),
roughly torn

2 shallots, sliced into
thin rings

¼ cup melted unsalted
butter or extra-virgin
olive oil

2 tablespoons sesame
seeds

1 teaspoon red chile
flakes

2 teaspoons kosher salt

While at university, I often found myself in the side streets of Sydney's Chinatown, slurping spicy ramen between classes. Twenty years later, I was delighted to find that my kids were equally excited by this delicious, umami-packed soup, but I was less thrilled to discover they were buying it in artificial ingredient-filled packets from the grocery store after school. As a busy mum, I fully understand the convenience of store-bought ramen, but making it from scratch from time to time also feels so satisfying and is surprisingly easy. Don't be put off by the long list of ingredients in this ramen-inspired recipe—it doesn't take long to prepare and includes many ingredients that may already be in your pantry.

1  **Make the broth:** In a large stock pot, combine the vegetable broth, water, soy sauce, miso, vinegar, garlic, and ginger and bring to a simmer over medium heat. Turn the heat down to medium-low and continue simmering until the broth is fragrant, 20 minutes. Stir in the tahini. Taste and add salt, if desired. Remove from the heat and set aside.

2  **Make the ramen:** Preheat the oven to 400°F. Line two rimmed baking sheets with parchment paper.

3  If using the Japanese eggplant, slice them in half lengthwise, then use a sharp knife to score the flat sides 3 or 4 times, and place cut-side down on one of the prepared baking sheets. For the regular eggplant, place the rounds directly on the prepared baking sheet. Drizzle with the vegetable oil and roast until the eggplant is lightly browned, about 25 minutes. Remove the baking sheet from the oven to let the eggplant cool slightly while leaving the oven on.

4  Add the mushrooms, shallots, butter, sesame seeds, red chile flakes, and 1 teaspoon of the salt to the other prepared baking sheet and toss to combine. Roast until the mushrooms are browned, about 15 minutes, shaking the pan halfway through. Switch the oven to broil, and broil for 1 to 2 minutes, until crisp. Watch closely so they don't burn. Remove from the oven and set aside.

5  Return the broth to the stove and bring to a boil over high heat. As soon as the broth comes to a boil, remove the pot from the heat. Stir in the ramen noodle squares and greens, then cover the pot with a lid and let sit until the noodles have softened, about 5 minutes. Taste the broth and add the remaining 1 teaspoon salt, if necessary.

6  **To serve:** Ladle the soup into four bowls. Top each bowl with equal amounts of the eggplant and crispy mushrooms, 1 soft-boiled egg (if using), scallions, and 1 tablespoon chili crisp (if using). Serve immediately. The ramen is best eaten on the day it's prepared.

4 packaged ramen noodle squares (about 95g per square)

4 cups chopped leafy greens (such as snow pea shoots, spinach, kale, bok choy, or gai lan)

4 soft-boiled eggs, cut in half, for serving (optional)

2 scallions, white and green parts thinly sliced

4 tablespoons chili crisp (optional)

# Polenta-Dusted Baked Sweet Potato Fries

—

*Serves 6 to 8*
*Time: 50 minutes*

3 large sweet potatoes, sliced into thin wedges, about ½ inch thick

2 tablespoons extra-virgin olive oil

1 tablespoon polenta

1 teaspoon kosher salt

Freshly ground pepper

1 tablespoon Gomasio (page 57; optional)

Tahini Miso Sauce, for serving (page 62)

This dish has a nice balance of bold, complex flavor from the tahini miso dipping sauce and a crispy texture from the polenta crust. Depending on what's available or in season, I like to use a mix of sweet potatoes and colored yams, as the color variation looks pretty on the plate! I always leave the skin on when I roast potatoes, even with the polenta dusting.

1  Preheat the oven to 400°F. Line a large rimmed baking sheet with parchment paper.

2  In a large bowl, combine the sweet potatoes, olive oil, polenta, salt, and a few grinds of pepper and toss to coat the wedges evenly.

3  Spread the sweet potatoes on the prepared baking sheet, making sure to allow space between each wedge so they crisp rather than steam.

4  Roast until brown and crispy, flipping the potatoes halfway through, about 45 minutes.

5  Sprinkle with the Gomasio (if using) and serve immediately alongside the Tahini Miso Sauce. The sauce may be prepared in advance and stored in an airtight container in the refrigerator for up to 3 days. The fries are best eaten on the day they're prepared.

# Crispy Mushrooms on Garlic Toast

—

*Serves 4*
*Time: 25 minutes*

—

2 tablespoons tahini

2 tablespoons extra-virgin olive oil, plus more as needed

1 tablespoon soy sauce

1 teaspoon maple syrup

1 pound maitake mushrooms, well cleaned (see Note)

1 tablespoon sesame seeds

4 thick slices sourdough bread or another fresh bread

1 garlic clove, sliced in half, skin on

1 cup labneh

1 handful leafy greens (such as snow pea shoots or arugula)

Flaky salt

Freshly ground pepper

—

**Note:** *If you can't find maitake mushrooms, oyster mushrooms are a good substitute.*

I recently took a girls' trip to Copenhagen with five friends, each flying in from a different city, each from a different chapter of my life, but all sharing my passion for travel and food. Of course, the entire weekend was planned around where we would be eating! One highlight was a little spot in the Kødbyen neighborhood, where we ordered lion's mane mushrooms on toast. It was such a unique dish that as soon as I returned to New York, I set about re-creating my own version. I used maitake mushrooms as they are slightly easier to find, but I also love the way so much extra flavor gets trapped in all their little nooks and crannies. There's plenty of research about the medicinal benefits of mushrooms. But, for me, the best form of medicine is time with friends, sharing a plate of simple food.

1   In a large bowl, whisk together the tahini, olive oil, soy sauce, and maple syrup. Set aside.

2   Using your hands, break the mushrooms into 1- to 2-inch pieces and add them to the bowl with the tahini mixture. Add the sesame seeds and gently toss the mixture until the mushrooms are evenly coated. You can prepare the mushrooms up to 1 hour in advance.

3   Heat 1 to 2 tablespoons of olive oil in a large skillet over high heat. Drain any excess marinade from the mushrooms, then add them to the pan and cook, turning once or twice, until the mushrooms are slightly caramelized but not burnt on the edges, about 5 minutes.

4   While the mushrooms are browning, toast the bread. Once the bread is toasted and still warm, rub the cut side of the garlic clove vigorously along the sharp, crusty edges of the bread.

5   Spread ¼ cup of the labneh on each piece of toast, then top with the leafy greens, a generous pile of mushrooms, and a drizzle of olive oil and tahini. Finish it off with a pinch of flaky salt and freshly ground pepper. This is best eaten on the day it's prepared.

If you ask me what my last supper would include, this dish would absolutely make the list. It features a combination of some of my favorite ingredients: lemon, Parmesan, garlic, and butter. I've been making this dish for weeknight dinners for more than twenty years, especially on Mondays as it's a good way to use up any sesame bagels or baguettes left over from the weekend.

# Lemony Orecchiette with Sesame Pangrattato

—

*Serves 4*
*Time: 30 minutes*

1  **Make the pangrattato:** In a small saucepan, melt the butter over medium-high heat until it starts to bubble. Reduce the heat to low and add the olive oil (this stops the butter from burning). Add the bread and stir until golden brown, 4 to 5 minutes. Add the lemon zest, sesame seeds, and salt and stir until well combined. Remove from the heat and set aside to cool.

2  **Make the pasta:** Bring a large saucepan of water to a boil. Add a generous pinch of salt and cook the pasta until al dente according to package instructions.

3  While the water comes to a boil, remove the hard woody end of the broccoli stem and discard. Thinly slice the rest of the stem into ¼-inch discs. Remove the florets from the stem, and cut them into small pieces so that they cook evenly with the discs.

4  While the pasta cooks, melt the butter in a large skillet over high heat. Reduce the heat to low and add the broccoli, garlic, and salt. Cook until the broccoli has started to char slightly, 2 to 3 minutes. Add 2 tablespoons of the pasta cooking water, then cover the skillet with a lid and steam the broccoli until tender, about 3 minutes.

5  When the pasta is ready, reserve ¼ cup of the cooking water and drain the pasta. Add the pasta to the skillet with the broccoli and toss well to combine.

6  Add the Parmesan, lemon juice, jalapeño (if using), and the reserved pasta water. Stir to combine.

7  Divide the pasta evenly among four bowls and finish with a heaping spoon of the pangrattato, a grind of pepper, a drizzle of the olive oil, and more Parmesan, if desired. The pasta can be stored in an airtight container in the refrigerator for up to 3 days and reheated before serving.

### For the pangrattato

1 tablespoon salted butter

1 tablespoon extra-virgin olive oil

1 baguette or 2 bagels, torn into pea-size pieces

Zest of 1 large lemon

1 tablespoon lightly toasted sesame seeds (see page 17)

½ teaspoon kosher salt

### For the pasta

8 ounces orecchiette or any other pasta shape

1 pound broccoli

2 tablespoons salted butter

4 garlic cloves, minced

½ teaspoon kosher salt, plus more for the pasta water

1 cup grated Parmesan, plus more for serving

Juice of 1 large lemon

1 small jalapeño, thinly sliced (optional)

Freshly ground pepper

Extra-virgin olive oil for drizzling

# Mushroom Köfte B'Siniyah

—

*Serves 4*
*Time: 1 hour, plus*
*chilling time*

**For the köfte**

4 tablespoons
extra-virgin olive oil

1 medium onion,
finely diced

1½ teaspoons ground
cumin

1 teaspoon ground
coriander

1½ teaspoons kosher salt

1 small eggplant, or
½ large eggplant, diced

¾ pound portobello
mushrooms, finely diced

4 garlic cloves, minced

1 cup breadcrumbs
(panko work well here)

3 eggs, lightly beaten

½ cup finely chopped
flat-leaf parsley

½ teaspoon ground
pepper

1 large bunch Tuscan
kale, stems removed and
leaves torn, or English
spinach, stems removed
and leaves left whole

¼ cup sesame seeds

Köfte, otherwise known as Middle Eastern meatballs, are traditionally made with beef or lamb. (You will sometimes see köfte referred to as kofta or küfte.) The word "köfte" originates from a cooking technique for grinding meat and dates back hundreds of years to the Ottoman Empire. I was curious to see how this dish might work with a vegetable base of mushrooms and eggplant. To me, it feels equally indulgent and is a good vegetarian alternative to the original. The mushroom köfte are served in a pool of creamy tahini sauce and topped with golden pine nuts and a sprinkling of fresh herbs. Serve stuffed inside a fresh pita to soak up the sauce.

1  **Make the köfte:** In a large ovenproof skillet, heat 3 tablespoons of the olive oil over medium heat. Add the onion and cook until slightly translucent, about 3 minutes. Stir in the cumin, coriander, and ½ teaspoon of the salt and cook for 1 minute. Add the eggplant, mushrooms, and garlic and cook until the mixture has started to brown and dehydrate, 10 minutes more.

2  Transfer the eggplant mixture to a large bowl and let it cool for 1 to 2 minutes. Add the breadcrumbs, eggs, parsley, and pepper and stir until well combined. Cover the bowl with plastic wrap and let the mixture firm up in the refrigerator for at least 1 hour or up to overnight.

3  When ready to cook, preheat the oven to 400°F.

4  In the same skillet you used for the eggplant, heat the remaining 1 tablespoon olive oil over high heat. Add the kale and the remaining 1 teaspoon salt and cook until the greens have just wilted, 1 to 2 minutes. Remove the skillet from the heat, leaving the greens in the pan, and use a wooden spoon to evenly spread the greens across the bottom of the skillet.

5  Place the sesame seeds in a shallow bowl. Remove the chilled eggplant mixture from the fridge and use your hands to roll 10 to 12 golf ball–size köfte. Roll each köfte in the sesame seeds, then place it on top of the wilted greens, leaving a little space between each köfte, if possible (this will help the köfte crisp up fully in the oven). Bake the köfte for 3 to 4 minutes.

*Continued*

## Mushroom Köfte B'Siniyah

—

*continued*

### For the sauce

1 cup tahini

1 cup water, plus more as needed

Zest and juice of 1½ lemons

1 teaspoon kosher salt, plus more as needed

1 teaspoon freshly ground pepper, plus more as needed

### For serving

1 tablespoon toasted pine nuts

1 tablespoon mint leaves

1 teaspoon Sumac Sesame Salt (page 57; optional)

Fresh pita

6  **Make the sauce:** While the köfte bakes, whisk together the tahini, water, lemon zest, lemon juice, salt, and pepper in a medium bowl. If the sauce seizes, add more water until you have a thick but pourable consistency.

7  Remove the skillet from the oven and pour the sauce around (not over the top of) the köfte, making sure to leave about half to two-thirds of each köfte exposed.

8  Return the skillet to the oven and bake until the top of each köfte has browned and the sauce is bubbling, 3 to 4 minutes. If desired, place the skillet under the broiler for 1 minute to crisp up the tops of each köfte even more.

9  Garnish with the pine nuts, mint, and Sumac Sesame Salt, if desired, then serve directly from the skillet with the fresh pita for scooping and dipping. The köfte mixture can be prepared up to 3 days in advance, but once combined with the sauce, it should be eaten the same day.

I've heard people describe cabbage as a blank canvas for layering flavor, which I wholeheartedly agree with. For this recipe, I wanted a combination of sweet, spicy, and acidic flavors, all brought together by creamy tahini that almost functions as an emulsifier. You can use any type of cabbage for this dish (green or red), but I especially love the pretty leaves of a Savoy cabbage if you can find one. Enjoy this dish as a simple yet hearty winter meal, or serve it as a side to a protein or couscous.

1  **Make the cabbage:** Cut the cabbage into 5 or 6 wedges, slicing lengthwise through the core. Cut out the tough inner core and discard.

2  In a large ovenproof skillet (I use a Le Creuset braiser), heat 2 tablespoons of the olive oil over medium-high heat. Brush each side of the cabbage with 1 to 2 tablespoons of the remaining olive oil, season with a sprinkle of salt and pepper, and place the cabbage in the skillet, cut-side down. Cook until charred on each side, 4 to 5 minutes per side. Be careful when turning the cabbage to retain the shape of the wedge. Transfer the cabbage to a plate. Set aside.

3  Preheat the oven to 375°F.

4  In the same skillet, warm 1 to 2 tablespoons of the remaining olive oil over medium heat. Add the shallots, 1 teaspoon salt, and several grinds of pepper and cook, stirring occasionally, until the shallots start to caramelize, 3 to 4 minutes. Add the lemon wedges and cook until the lemons start to take on a slightly golden color, 2 to 3 minutes.

5  Increase the heat to high and pour the broth, vinegar, and orange juice over the shallots and lemon wedges. As soon as it starts to boil, transfer 2 to 3 tablespoons of this braising liquid to a small bowl and set aside, then turn the heat off and gently return the cabbage wedges to the skillet.

6  Cover the skillet with a lid, transfer it to the oven, and roast for 30 minutes, turning the cabbage wedges once halfway through.

# Skillet-Roasted Cabbage with Caramelized Shallots, Citrus & Tahini

—

*Serves 4 as a side or
2 as a main course*

*Time: 45 minutes*

**For the cabbage**

1 large cabbage

4 to 6 tablespoons extra-virgin olive oil

Kosher salt for seasoning, plus 1 teaspoon

Freshly ground pepper

4 medium shallots, peeled and cut lengthwise into quarters

1 lemon, cut lengthwise into quarters

1 cup vegetable or chicken broth

¼ cup white wine vinegar

Juice of 1 orange

1 cup uncooked Israeli couscous (optional)

2 tablespoons coarsely chopped roasted, salted almonds

*Continued*

Skillet-Roasted
Cabbage with
Caramelized
Shallots, Citrus &
Tahini

—

*continued*

**For the sauce**

Zest of 1 orange

½ cup tahini, plus more
if needed

¼ cup water, plus more
if needed

1 tablespoon maple syrup

1 teaspoon kosher salt,
plus more as needed

½ teaspoon red chile
flakes

Freshly ground pepper

7   While the cabbage is braising, prepare the couscous according to the package instructions (if using).

8   **Make the tahini sauce:** In a medium bowl, whisk the reserved braising liquid, orange zest, tahini, water, maple syrup, salt, red chile flakes, and several grinds of pepper. The sauce should have a pourable consistency. If it's too thick, add more water. If it's too thin, add 1 to 2 more tablespoons tahini. Taste for seasoning and add more salt and pepper, if desired.

9   When ready to serve, spread the tahini sauce on a platter and top with the couscous (if using), cabbage wedges, shallots, lemon wedges, almonds, and a few grinds of pepper. You can also serve the cabbage wedges at the table straight out of the skillet with a bowl of the tahini sauce on the side. The sauce can be prepared up to 3 days in advance. The cabbage and couscous is best eaten on the day it's made.

A couple of days before I was due to turn in my manuscript for this book, I was chatting with an old Aussie friend, Jane—a kindred spirit, cookbook obsessive, and fellow foodie trapped in the body of a corporate lawyer. As we were exchanging ideas about ways to include sesame in our cooking, Jane began to rave to me about a technique she had recently discovered for cooking fried eggs with a crispy sesame crust. I gave this technique a try and decided it was a worthy last minute addition to this book. Served over a bowl of riced cauliflower or fried rice, this dish makes for an easy weeknight meal.

# Sesame-Crusted Eggs with Cauliflower Fried Rice

—

*Serves 2*
*Time: 25 minutes*

1   **Make the cauliflower rice:** In a large wok or large skillet, heat the oil over medium heat. Add the carrot and cook until starting to soften, 2 to 3 minutes. Add the garlic, ginger, and three-quarters of the scallions and cook for 2 to 3 minutes more. Add the cauliflower and cook, stirring frequently, until it begins to brown slightly, 2 to 3 minutes.

2   Reduce the heat to low and add the hoisin sauce, soy sauce, sesame oil, and cashews. Stir to combine and let sit while you make the eggs.

3   **Make the eggs:** In a large nonstick skillet, melt the butter over medium-high heat. When it starts to bubble, add the olive oil. Sprinkle in ½ cup of the sesame seeds in the shape of two 4-inch circles.

4   Carefully break an egg over each sesame circle and sprinkle the remaining 2 teaspoons sesame seeds over each egg. Cook for 2 minutes, until the white part of the egg has set. For a firmer yolk, gently flip the egg and cook for another minute.

5   To serve, divide the rice evenly between two bowls, slide an egg over the top, and finish with the chili crisp (if using), cilantro, and the remaining scallions.

—

Note: *Ready-to-cook riced cauliflower is available at most grocery stores and online. Alternatively, you can use 3 cups of the cooked rice of your choosing. Treat it as you would the riced cauliflower, adding at the end of step 1.*

**For the rice**

2 to 3 tablespoons vegetable oil

1 large carrot, diced

2 garlic cloves, minced

1-inch piece fresh ginger, grated

1 bunch scallions, green and white parts thinly sliced

1 pound riced cauliflower (see Note)

1 tablespoon hoisin sauce

1 tablespoon soy sauce

1 tablespoon lightly toasted sesame oil

½ cup salted toasted cashews, coarsely chopped

**For the eggs**

½ tablespoon unsalted butter

1 tablespoon olive oil

½ cup plus 2 teaspoons sesame seeds

2 eggs

2 tablespoons chili crisp or spicy tahini (optional)

2 tablespoons roughly torn fresh cilantro

# Green on Green on Green

—

*Serves 3 to 4 as a side dish or 1 as a main course*

*Time: 20 minutes*

—

2 pounds broccolini or sliced broccoli with stems

1 bunch kale, stems removed

2 tablespoons extra-virgin olive oil, plus more for drizzling

Kosher salt

Spicy Green Tahini Sauce (page 63; see Note), cut limes reserved after juicing (optional)

2 tablespoons Savory Dukkah (page 54) or lightly toasted sesame seeds (see page 17)

—

**Note:** *I like the Spicy Green Tahini Sauce here, but any of the sauces from pages 62 to 63 will be delicious with this dish.*

I absolutely adore this dish! Just thinking about the layers of charred greens over a spicy, tangy green tahini sauce makes my taste buds tingle. But, like all great relationships, this dish is just as delicious on its own as it is partnered up with a grilled protein or ancient grain like cooked farro or freekeh.

1  Preheat the oven to 375°F. Line a rimmed baking sheet with parchment paper.

2  Spread the broccolini and kale evenly over the prepared baking sheet, being careful not to crowd the pan (use two pans if necessary). Add the olive oil and a pinch of salt, tossing to coat. Roast until the vegetables start to char, 8 minutes.

3  An optional but delicious step: Heat a small skillet over high heat and place one of the reserved lime halves cut-side down in the pan and sear until slightly caramelized and charred, 2 minutes. Reserve for garnish and a potential last drop of juice to be squeezed over the greens.

4  When ready to serve, swoosh some of the sauce over a plate, then add the greens, Savory Dukkah, and a drizzle of olive oil. Squeeze any remaining juice from the charred lime over everything, then add as a garnish to the finished plate.

# Crispy Tofu with Bok Choy & Soba

———

*Serves 2 to 3*
*Time: 20 minutes*

A bowl of crispy tofu with stir-fried greens and steamed rice or soba noodles is my family's favorite weeknight meal. The secret to the perfect crisp coating is a light dusting of seasoned cornstarch. My other tip is to make sure you're using the right tofu. Firm tofu tends to taste rubbery when fried and silken tofu will fall apart, but medium-firm (well-pressed) tofu will be just right. As a reward for helping in the kitchen, my kids have usually stolen half of the extra-crispy tofu chunks before the dish even hits the table! Serve with rice, cauliflower rice, or soba noodles, like the recipe here.

**For the bok choy & toppings**

1 tablespoon vegetable oil

5 baby bok choy, halved lengthwise, or 1 pound snow pea leaves

2 garlic cloves, minced

½ teaspoon kosher salt

2 tablespoons water

1 scallion, green and white parts thinly sliced

**For the tofu**

⅓ cup cornstarch

1 tablespoon five-spice powder

1 teaspoon kosher salt

1 (14-ounce) block medium-firm tofu, drained and pressed

½ cup vegetable oil

**For the sauce**

½ cup tahini

¼ cup water, plus more as needed

1 teaspoon shoyu or soy sauce

1 tablespoon honey

1   **Make the bok choy:** In a large skillet, heat the oil over medium heat. Add the bok choy, garlic, and salt and cook until soft or just cooked through, 2 to 3 minutes. Do not let the garlic burn. Add the water, cover the skillet with a lid, and remove from the heat. Let the bok choy sit for a few minutes more to wilt.

2   **Make the tofu:** In a shallow bowl, combine the cornstarch, five-spice powder, and salt.

3   Pat the tofu dry with paper towels and cut into 1-inch cubes. Transfer the tofu to the bowl with the cornstarch mixture and carefully dredge the cubes until they're coated on all sides.

4   In a large nonstick skillet, warm the oil over medium-high heat and line a large plate with paper towels. Once the oil is very hot, and working in batches if necessary, add the tofu to the skillet and fry, using a slotted spoon to turn the tofu every so often until golden, 4 to 6 minutes. Transfer the tofu cubes to the prepared plate to drain.

5   **Make the sauce:** In a small bowl, combine the tahini, water, shoyu, honey, vinegar, and chili crisp and whisk until smooth, adding more water, as needed, to loosen. Add 2 tablespoons of the sauce to the bok choy and toss to combine.

6  To serve, place the soba noodles on a platter, drizzle with the remaining sauce, pile on the bok choy and tofu, and sprinkle the scallions over top. Drizzle with more chili crisp, if desired, and serve immediately.

1 tablespoon rice vinegar

1 tablespoon chili crisp, plus more for drizzling

1 (8-ounce) package soba noodles, cooked according to instructions

# Chicken for Lemon Lovers with Tarator

—

*Serves 4*
*Time: 1 hour*

8 bone-in, skin-on chicken thighs

1 tablespoon kosher salt

Freshly ground pepper

¼ cup extra-virgin olive oil, plus 1 tablespoon for searing

2 lemons, zested and sliced into rounds

½ teaspoon turmeric (optional)

3 shallots, sliced into rings

### Tarator & toppings

Walnut Tahini Tarator (page 62), at room temperature

2 tablespoons toasted walnuts, coarsely chopped (optional)

1 to 2 tablespoons black and white sesame seeds, for garnish

This is a flavorful, tangy, super-satisfying dish. It's great for a casual lunch or dinner but works equally well for entertaining, given how gorgeous all the colors will look at your table. Once plated, the tarator sauce will start to meld into the chicken juices, so make sure to serve it with a side of roasted potatoes, rice, or couscous to slurp up all that flavor! I often add a little ground turmeric to give the chicken a pretty golden color, but you can omit it if you'd like. The sauce can be made two days in advance and kept in the fridge.

1 Preheat the oven to 375°F.

2 Pat the chicken dry with a paper towel. Transfer to a medium bowl and combine with the salt, several grinds of pepper, ¼ cup of the olive oil, lemon zest, and turmeric (if using). Use your hands to toss the chicken pieces in the seasoning until coated (wear gloves or wash your hands immediately after this step or they will be stained by the turmeric).

3 In a large skillet, heat the remaining 1 tablespoon olive oil over medium-high heat. Place the chicken thighs in the oil skin-side down and cook until the skin has started to brown, 2 to 3 minutes. Transfer the chicken to a plate and set aside.

4 Line a rimmed baking sheet with parchment paper. Spread out the shallots and lemon rounds evenly and top with the chicken thighs skin-side up. Cover the sheet with aluminum foil and roast for 25 to 30 minutes. Remove the foil and roast for 5 to 10 minutes more to give the chicken a crispier skin.

5 To serve, place the chicken, lemon rounds, and shallots on a bed of rice or couscous and pour any pan baking juices over the top. Drizzle the Walnut Tahini Tarator over the chicken and garnish with the walnuts and a sprinkle of black and white sesame seeds. This dish will keep in an airtight container in the refrigerator for up to 3 days and is best reheated, covered in foil, in the oven.

Whenever radishes are in season, I love to admire their intense color and artistic beauty. I must admit I don't eat them particularly often, though, because I'm never quite sure what to do with them beyond occasionally throwing them in a salad. But I was inspired by my friend Susan Spungen to try roasting them after reading a recipe in her newsletter, *Susanality*. I was hooked! The caramelization brings out the sweetness of the radishes and tames some of their peppery zip. The intense, tangy, briny sauce in this recipe stands up to the peppery punch of the radishes with gusto. This recipe yields more sauce than is needed for the radishes, but it will keep covered in the fridge for up to five days, ready to be smothered over crusty bread or drizzled over any other fresh or roasted vegetable dish.

1  Preheat the oven to 400°F. Line a rimmed baking sheet with parchment paper.

2  **Make the radishes:** In a medium bowl, toss the radishes with the olive oil, salt, and a few grinds of pepper. Add the radishes to the prepared baking sheet, making sure to spread them out as much as possible. Roast until the radishes have softened and the edges start to crisp, 40 to 45 minutes.

3  **Make the sauce:** While the radishes are roasting, heat the anchovy-tin oil in a small saucepan over high heat. Add the anchovy fillets—I include 3, but use all 6 if you love their taste— and the garlic and immediately reduce the heat to low. Cook until the anchovies have melted, 3 to 4 minutes. The mixture should now look like a paste. Set aside to cool slightly.

4  In a food processor or large bowl with a whisk, combine the tahini, water, lemon juice, and vinegar and blend until smooth. If the sauce is too thick, mix in 1 to 2 tablespoons more water.

5  Add the anchovy mixture from the saucepan to the blender, and blend until smooth. Taste and season with salt and pepper, if needed.

6  To serve, spread the sauce on a plate and top with a pile of the radishes. Scatter the chives over top, if desired, and serve immediately.

# Roasted Radishes

143

—

*Serves 4 to 6*
*Time: 50 minutes*

**For the radishes**

3 bunches radishes (the more colors, the better!), trimmed with ½ inch of stem left on, halved

2 to 3 tablespoons extra-virgin olive oil

1 teaspoon kosher salt

Freshly ground pepper

**For the sauce**

3 to 6 anchovy fillets packed in oil, 2 tablespoons oil reserved

2 garlic cloves, minced

¾ cup tahini

⅓ cup cold water, plus more as needed

Juice of 1 lemon

1 tablespoon white wine vinegar or another vinegar

Kosher salt and freshly ground pepper

½ cup finely chopped fresh chives or whole microgreens

# Miso & Marmalade Arctic Char with Soba

—

*Serves 4*
*Time: 20 minutes*

**For the fish and glaze**

2 tablespoons white miso

2 tablespoons marmalade

1 teaspoon sesame oil

1½ tablespoons water

½ teaspoon kosher salt

One 1½-pound arctic char fillet, skin on

**For the noodles**

2½ tablespoons tahini

2 tablespoons rice vinegar

2 tablespoons water, plus more if needed

1½ tablespoons soy sauce

1 tablespoon mirin

8 ounces soba noodles

8 ounces snow peas, thinly sliced

½ bunch cilantro, leaves and stems finely chopped

4 scallions, green and white parts thinly sliced

1 medium cucumber, thinly sliced

1 tablespoon Furikake (page 57) or a mixture of black and lightly toasted white sesame seeds (see page 17)

During a recent trip to Australia, I spent time with my childhood friend Anna and her husband, Steve, who worked for decades in some of the world's most celebrated Michelin-starred restaurants. The phrase "backbreaking work" couldn't be more apt to describe a career in professional kitchens, and by the time Steve reached his forties, he needed a less physically demanding profession and went back to school to train as a therapist. Whether he's a chef or therapist, I've always turned to Steve for kitchen-related moral support! It was Steve who suggested adding marmalade to this recipe, which I thought was genius. It caramelizes under the broiler, forming the most delicious sweet crust for the fish.

1  Place a large rimmed baking sheet in the oven and preheat to 425°F.

2  **Make the glaze:** In a small bowl, whisk the miso, marmalade, and sesame oil. Add the water and salt and whisk to combine.

3  Place the fish on a large plate, skin-side down. Using a pastry brush or the back of a spoon, coat the flesh with the glaze.

4  When ready to roast, place the glazed fish skin-side down on the preheated baking sheet, and return it immediately to the oven. Roast until the glaze is darkly caramelized and bubbling and the fish flakes easily, 12 minutes. If it looks like it is burning toward the end of the cooking time, loosely tent aluminum foil over the top of the fish.

5  **Make the noodles:** In a large bowl, whisk the tahini, vinegar, 2 tablespoons of the water, the soy sauce, and the mirin to combine. Set aside.

6  Cook the soba noodles according to the package instructions, then transfer to the bowl with the sauce and toss to combine. Add the snow peas, cilantro, scallions, cucumber, and Furikake and gently mix to combine.

7  Divide the noodles among four bowls and top with flaked pieces of the arctic char.

This recipe was inspired by an unassuming yet wildly popular restaurant, Fiorioni's, tucked away in the small country town of Orange, Australia, four hours west of Sydney. Their signature rainbow trout is always on the menu, but you need to get your order in early before they sell out. Serve the trout with a simple side of roasted potatoes or rice, letting the fish be the star of the show.

1 **Prepare the fish:** If you have time, leave the fish uncovered in the fridge for up to 24 hours prior to roasting. This will help dry out the fish so the skin crisps up in the oven.

2 When ready to roast, preheat the oven to 450°F and place a large rimmed baking sheet in the oven about 5 minutes before roasting.

3 Pat each trout thoroughly with a paper towel, making sure the fish is completely dry. Using a sharp knife, slash each side of the trout two to three times.

4 Sprinkle the flour and salt over a plate and give it a quick stir to combine. Roll each fish in the flour to lightly coat all sides.

5 Fill the cavity of each fish with the lime slices.

6 Remove the preheated baking sheet from the oven and drizzle it with 2 tablespoons of the olive oil. Immediately place the fish on the baking sheet (it should sizzle slightly), then drizzle more olive oil over each fish.

7 Return the baking sheet to the oven and immediately reduce the temperature to 375°F. Roast the fish until cooked through, 15 to 20 minutes.

8 **Make the relish:** In a small bowl, whisk the soy sauce, sesame oil, ginger, lime juice, and shallots. Add the avocado, cilantro, cucumber, jalapeño, and sesame seeds, and gently toss together. Do not overmix or the avocado will get mushy.

9 Serve the fish with the relish piled over the top or alongside.

—

Note: *Select an avocado that is ripe but still slightly firm. This way, it won't get too soft when you try to dice it.*

# Oven-Roasted Trout with Spicy Avocado Relish

—

*Serves 2*
*Time: 30 minutes*

**For the fish**

2 whole rainbow trout or Branzino, gutted and scaled

3 tablespoons all-purpose flour

1 tablespoon kosher salt

1 lime, thinly sliced into rounds

2 tablespoons extra-virgin olive oil, plus more for drizzling

**For the relish**

2 tablespoons soy sauce

1 tablespoon sesame oil

1 tablespoon finely grated fresh ginger

Juice of 1 lime

1 small shallot, finely diced

1 avocado, diced (see Note)

½ bunch cilantro, finely chopped

1 medium Lebanese cucumber, diced

1 jalapeño, thinly sliced

1 tablespoon sesame seeds

# Gomasio-Crusted Salmon Skewers

—

*Makes 8 skewers*
*Time: 15 minutes, plus*
*30 minutes to marinate*

¼ cup sake

¼ cup soy sauce

¼ cup mirin

2 teaspoons brown sugar

1 tablespoon sesame oil

2½ pounds salmon,
cut into 2-inch cubes

1 pint cherry tomatoes
(in summer, I love to use
a mix of sungolds and
regular cherry tomatoes)

3 tablespoons Gomasio
(page 57; see Note), plus
more for garnish

1 teaspoon cornstarch

—

Note: *You can substitute the*
*gomasio with 3 tablespoons*
*sesame seeds with*
*1 tablespoon flaky salt.*

The flavors in this recipe were inspired by a dish at a local sushi restaurant near my home in Chelsea, New York, famous for their salmon sushi topped with a broiled tomato. It literally melts in your mouth and is the most popular item on the menu. You can make this dish with any type of fleshy white fish, including halibut, sea bass, and mahi mahi. It's helpful if you have a fishmonger cut the fish into 2-inch cubes so the skewers can be assembled quickly. Serve with Japanese Cabbage Salad (page 106) and a bowl of steamed rice.

1  In a large bowl, whisk the sake, soy sauce, mirin, and brown sugar until the sugar has dissolved. Whisk in the sesame oil.

2  Add the fish to the marinade and toss until well coated. Cover and refrigerate for at least 30 minutes and up to 4 hours. If you are using bamboo skewers, you will need to soak them in cold water for at least 30 minutes, or preferably overnight in the refrigerator, before using them. The soaking prevents the skewers from burning while on the grill. Metal skewers don't require this step.

3  When ready to grill, remove the fish from the fridge and add the tomatoes to the bowl, tossing to coat in the marinade.

4  Thread the fish and tomatoes onto the skewers, alternating between the two.

5  Preheat a grill pan or outdoor grill to medium-high, or preheat a broiler if you prefer to cook your skewers in the oven.

6  Just prior to placing the skewers on the grill, combine the Gomasio and cornstarch on a large plate. Lightly coat each skewer in the mixture (the cornstarch will give the skewer a very light crispy edge).

7  Grill the skewers, turning halfway so that the fish doesn't burn, for about 3 minutes per side. If using a broiler, cook the skewers for 10 minutes, turning halfway through, while watching closely so they don't burn.

8  Sprinkle the skewers with more Gomasio, if desired, and serve immediately.

These grilled zucchini ribbons add a sophisticated bite to any summer barbecue menu. To transform this into a more substantial dish, serve the skewers alongside a bowl of couscous or use the zucchini and sauce to fill a pita!

1  **Make the zucchini:** If you are using bamboo skewers, you will need to soak them in cold water for at least 30 minutes, or preferably overnight in the refrigerator, before using them. The soaking prevents the skewers from burning while on the grill. Metal skewers don't require this step.

2  Cut the ends off the zucchinis. Leave the skin on and use a vegetable peeler or mandoline to shave the zucchini lengthwise and create ribbons about ⅛ inch thick.

3  In a large bowl, toss the ribbons with the olive oil, za'atar, salt, and pepper until evenly coated.

4  Working with one at a time, fold the ribbons in alternating directions into an accordion shape, then slide a skewer through the center and place it on a plate until ready for the grill (you can make these a few hours ahead and refrigerate until ready to grill).

5  Preheat a grill or grill pan over medium-high heat.

6  Grill the skewers until tender and charred on the edges, turning frequently so they don't burn, 6 to 8 minutes total. Place the lemon cut-side down on the grill and cook until slightly charred, 2 to 3 minutes.

7  **Make the sauce:** In a small bowl, whisk the tahini, ice water, yogurt, and a squeeze of juice from the grilled lemon. Season with salt and pepper. The mixture will slowly thicken up into a sauce as you whisk. If it seems too thick, add 1 to 2 tablespoons water, or if it's too thin, add 1 to 2 tablespoons tahini, whisking until the sauce has a luscious, velvety consistency.

8  To serve, swoosh the sauce (reserve 1 to 2 tablespoons for drizzling) over a serving platter.

9  Add the zucchini skewers to the center of the platter and finish with a final squeeze of the grilled lemon, a drizzle of olive oil, the reserved sauce, and a pinch of za'atar.

# Charred Za'atar Zucchini Skewers

—

*Serves 6*
*Time: 25 minutes*

**For the zucchini**

3 medium zucchinis

2 to 3 tablespoons extra-virgin olive oil, plus more for drizzling

1 tablespoon za'atar, plus more for garnish (see Note)

1 teaspoon kosher salt

1 teaspoon freshly ground pepper

1 lemon, halved

**For the tahini-yogurt sauce**

½ cup tahini, plus more as needed

⅓ cup ice water, plus more as needed

¼ cup plain Greek yogurt

Kosher salt and freshly ground pepper

—

**Note:** *Za'atar is available at most specialty stores and online.*

# Wok-Fried Greens

—

*Serves 2*
*Time: 15 minutes*

2 tablespoons rice syrup or maple syrup

1½ tablespoons red or white miso paste

4 garlic cloves, minced

1 teaspoon grated fresh ginger (from a 1-inch piece)

1 tablespoon soy sauce

1 tablespoon sesame oil

1 to 2 tablespoons water, plus more for frying

3 to 4 tablespoons vegetable oil

1½ pounds green beans, ends trimmed

½ pound asparagus, cut on the diagonal into 3-inch spears

1 teaspoon kosher salt

2 scallions, green and white parts sliced on the diagonal

1 tablespoon sesame seeds

1 teaspoon red chile flakes

This is another great clean-out-the-fridge style of dish. You can make this recipe using any or all of the green vegetables listed, depending on what you have available—sliced bok choy, broccoli florets, snow peas, or chopped kale make great additions. Just make sure that your vegetables are cut into roughly similar sizes so they cook at the same rate. Serve with grilled chicken or fish or the crispy tofu on page 138.

1  In a small bowl, whisk the rice syrup, miso, garlic, and ginger. Add the soy sauce, sesame oil, and water and stir until well combined. Set aside.

2  Heat the vegetable oil in a wok or large frying pan over high heat. When the vegetable oil is shimmering, add the green beans, asparagus, salt, and scallions, toss with tongs, and cook until the vegetables are almost tender and start to char, 2 to 3 minutes. If you prefer the vegetables slightly more tender, add 2 to 3 tablespoons water to the wok and cook for another minute.

3  Reduce the heat to medium, add the ginger soy sauce mixture to the wok, and toss until the vegetables are well coated and the sauce has started to bubble at the base of the wok. Add the sesame seeds and red chile flakes and give the wok a final toss. Check for seasoning and serve immediately. The vegetables can be stored in an airtight container in the refrigerator for up to 3 days and are best reheated in a wok or frying pan before serving.

Note: Shoyu is Japanese-style soy sauce. It can be purchased at well-stocked markets or online.

I met Ken at a gathering for food entrepreneurs in New York. As the next-generation owner of Sun Noodles, a forty-four-year-old ramen noodle business, Ken's thoughts on how to build a lasting company committed to quality food were invaluable to me. Ken's father, Hidehito Uki, was born in Japan and moved to Hawaii in 1980. He brought with him a passion for Japanese craftsmanship and an ambition to create noodles in the US as delicious as the ones he was used to in Japan.

This recipe was inspired by one of Ken's favorite childhood ramen spots, Gomaichi. He loved their ramen so much that he got a job there as dishwasher just so he could eat their ramen for staff meals, though he eventually worked his way from dishes to line cook. Ken has been trying to re-create this dish for years, testing iterations with gusto alongside his mom, Keiko, and wife, Naoko.

While this dish includes many components, it comes together very easily and quickly once you have the ingredients assembled. For a vegetarian option, replace the chicken stock with vegetable stock and the chicken with firm crumbled tofu.

1  **Make the soup and toppings:** In a medium nonstick skillet, warm the oil over medium-high heat. Add the garlic and ginger and cook until fragrant, about 2 minutes. Add the chicken and cook until cooked through and slightly browned, 4 to 5 minutes. Add the shoyu, mirin, and sugar and cook for 1 to 2 minutes more. Remove from the heat and set aside.

2  **Make the soup base:** In a medium saucepan, combine the chicken broth, shoyu, vinegar, chili oil, and bouillon powder. Stir and bring to a simmer over low heat and simmer until ready to serve.

3  When ready to serve, add 2 tablespoons to ¼ cup tahini to each soup bowl, depending on your taste. Pour ¼ cup of the soup base over the tahini and stir to combine. Divide the remaining soup broth and ramen noodles evenly between each bowl.

4  Top each portion with the chicken mixture, 1 egg, scallions, bok choy, and cashews.

5  Taste and adjust the seasoning as needed, finishing with a pinch of the Szechuan pepper if you'd like additional heat.

# Tan Tan Men Ramen

—

*Recipe shared by*
**Kenshiro Uki**

*Serves 2*
*Time: 40 minutes*

**For the soup and toppings**

2 tablespoons vegetable oil

1 garlic clove, finely minced

1 teaspoon minced fresh ginger (from a 1-inch piece)

½ pound ground chicken

1 tablespoon shoyu

1 teaspoon mirin

1 teaspoon sugar

10 ounces ramen noodles, cooked to package instructions

2 soft-boiled or hard-boiled eggs, halved

½ bunch scallions, green and white parts thinly sliced on the diagonal

½ pound bok choy, blanched

½ cup toasted cashews, coarsely chopped

Ground Szechuan pepper for serving (optional)

**For the soup base**

2½ cups chicken broth

½ cup shoyu

2 tablespoons rice vinegar

2 tablespoons chili oil or ½ teaspoon red chile flakes

1 teaspoon chicken bouillon powder

¼ to ½ cup tahini

# SOMETHING SWEET

# Tahini Salted Caramel Sauce

—

*Makes about 2 cups*
*Time: 20 minutes*

1 cup sugar

½ cup water

½ cup heavy cream, at room temperature (see Note)

2 tablespoons salted butter, cubed and at room temperature

½ cup tahini, at room temperature

1 teaspoon pure vanilla extract

1 teaspoon kosher salt

——

**Note:** *Make sure your ingredients are at room temperature as they may cause the caramel to seize if they are too cold.*

Just putting pen to paper for this recipe makes my taste buds tingle. I've always loved the combination of caramel and salt, but adding tahini gives an unmistakable depth of flavor—it's what takes this sauce from "yum" to sublime. Make a jar to keep in the fridge, taking it out whenever needed to spoon over ice cream and pancakes, add to a pie filling, or dollop into the center of the Triple Sesame Thumbprint Cookies on page 169. My daughter Annika's favorite after-school snack are apple slices drizzled with a spoon (or two or three!) of this sauce.

Making caramel takes a bit of practice, so I would encourage you to read the entire recipe before you start (see Note). The caramel will last for 2 to 3 months in an airtight container in the refrigerator.

1  In a very clean saucepan, warm the sugar and enough water to cover it over medium heat. Allow the sugar to slowly dissolve by continuously swirling the saucepan over the heat—don't be tempted to use a spoon to stir here.

2  Dip a pastry brush in the mixture and use it to wet down the sides of the saucepan, making sure there are no stray crystals of sugar that haven't been fully dissolved.

3  Once the sugar has melted and starts to bubble, allow it to cook, without stirring. Do not leave the saucepan unattended for too long. The sugar will start to turn golden when it's almost ready, and the fine line between an amber-colored, perfectly cooked caramel and a burnt, inedible mess is very easy to cross!

4  Once the sugar syrup is a deep, even golden brown (keep swirling the saucepan over the heat if the color isn't uniform), remove the saucepan from the heat and quickly add the cream and butter, stirring with a heat-safe spatula or wooden spoon until smooth (watch out for splatters!).

5  Add the tahini, vanilla, and salt and continue to stir until well combined. Do not worry if the mixture seizes a little at this stage.

*Continued*

*Sesame*

6 Return the saucepan to the stove and set over very low heat, stirring slowly until the caramel comes together and is completely smooth.

7 Pour the caramel into a clean glass jar or bowl and set aside to cool. Cover and keep at room temperature for up to a week or refrigerate for up to 3 months—warm it up in the microwave for a few seconds just before using.

—

Note: *This is the kind of recipe where you need to have all of your ingredients measured and ready to go before you start. For best results, make the caramel in a heavy stainless steel pan. I specifically purchased a saucepan without sharp corners at the base to help perfect this sauce, and while it's not essential, it was certainly helpful. Your biggest risk in making this sauce is that the sugar crystals don't melt evenly or catch on something in the pan, which will cause the sugar to crystalize and give this sauce an unwanted grainy texture—or as my dear friend Hanna likes to describe it, a "caramel disaster"!*

Tahini Salted
Caramel Sauce

—

*continued*

I developed this recipe with Kristin Nelson, one of the most humble, gracious women I've met. Kristin is the founder of The Ardent Homesteader, making jars of salted caramel near her farm in upstate New York. I first met Kristin while I was wandering through Williams Sonoma, where she was doing an in-store tasting. We struck up a conversation and immediately bonded over "mompreneur life" in the small artisan food world and how hard it was to put yourself—and your products—out into the world.

Of course, I immediately bought several jars of the salted caramel (a great decision) and went home to develop a tahini caramel popcorn recipe. After I first published this recipe, Kristin kindly called me to share that she had made my recipe but thought it needed some tweaking. Her version is an absolute winner and makes the most wonderful homemade holiday treat.

1  Preheat the oven to 250°F. Line a rimmed baking sheet with parchment paper.

2  If necessary, warm the caramel in the microwave for 30 seconds to get the consistency soft enough so that it can be easily stirred together with the tahini. In a small bowl, combine the caramel and tahini and stir until incorporated.

3  In a large bowl, toss the popcorn with the salt. Taste and add more salt if needed.

4  Drizzle some of the caramel mixture over the popcorn, using a spatula to toss until well coated. Continue pouring in the caramel mixture a little at a time, tossing well after each addition.

5  Spread the coated popcorn on the prepared baking sheet and bake for 1 hour, stirring with a heat-safe spatula every 15 minutes or so. Sprinkle the sesame seeds over the popcorn after 45 minutes of baking.

6  Place the baking sheet on a wire rack to cool completely. Store leftovers in an airtight container for up to 3 days.

# Tahini Caramel Popcorn

—

*Recipe shared by*
Kristin Nelson

*Makes 16 cups*
*Time: 1 hour*

1 cup Tahini Salted Caramel Sauce (page 158) or Kristin's Cara-Sel Caramel from theardenthomesteader.com

3 tablespoons tahini (see Note)

16 cups plain, unsalted popcorn (popped)

1½ teaspoons kosher salt, plus more as needed

2 tablespoons sesame seeds

—

Note: *Use only 1 tablespoon tahini if using the Tahini Salted Caramel Sauce recipe from page 158.*

This recipe was a real hit with our community when we first shared it, opening people's eyes to the idea that tahini and chocolate make an unexpected, yet truly divine, flavor friendship. This recipe became the catalyst for years of experimentation with tahini—I began using it as a substitute for butter or cream in many other dishes where I was looking for a dairy-free way to impart a creamy, luscious, texture. Serve these truffles at the end of a meal with coffee or peppermint tea so that they melt in your mouth.

1 Line a 9 by 5-inch loaf pan with parchment paper or plastic wrap.

2 Fill a saucepan or double boiler with about 1 inch of water and bring to a simmer over medium heat. Place the chocolate in a metal bowl and set the bowl over the simmering water, making sure the bottom of the bowl does not touch the water. Melt the chocolate, gently scraping down the sides of the bowl with a spatula as needed so the chocolate melts evenly. Alternatively, place the chocolate in a heat-safe bowl and microwave for 30-second intervals, stirring the chocolate after each burst until it's almost completely melted (it will continue to melt once you remove it from the microwave).

3 When the chocolate has completely melted, remove it from the heat. Use a rubber spatula to stir in the tahini.

4 Scrape the mixture into the prepared pan and refrigerate for at least 2 hours or overnight. You can also place it in the freezer, which will make it easier to slice with sharp edges.

5 When ready to serve, remove the chocolate from the pan and slice into cubes, rectangular logs, or any shape you like.

6 To finish, place some of the cocoa powder on a small plate. Coat each truffle in the cocoa and enjoy! Alternatively, store the truffles before dusting with cocoa in an airtight container in the refrigerator for up to 2 weeks or in the freezer for up to 2 months. Dust with cocoa just prior to serving.

# Tahini Truffles

—

*Makes 30 truffles*
*Time: 10 minutes,*
*plus 2 hours (or more) to set*

2 cups (about
9 ounces) chopped
70% dark chocolate

1½ cups tahini

Unsweetened Dutch-
process cocoa powder
(the best quality you
can find), for dusting

# Alegrías with Coconut & Anise

—

Recipe shared by
Mariana Velásquez

Makes 10 to 12
Time: 10 minutes

1 cup unsweetened coconut flakes

⅓ cup date syrup

⅓ cup tahini

2 teaspoons anise seeds

1 tablespoon sesame seeds

9 cups puffed millet (see Note) or unsalted popcorn (popped)

2 to 3 teaspoons flaky salt

—

**Note:** *Puffed millet, also known as peep corn, can be found online and at specialty health stores.*

I spied Mariana from across the room at a New York restaurant opening when I first moved to the city. Adorned in a vibrant, colorful dress accessorized by large, almost theatrical, vintage jewelry, she was unmissable. After Anna Polonsky, the restaurant designer responsible for our Chelsea Market store, introduced us, Mariana shared with me that she loved our halva, as it reminded her of her dad. While Mariana grew up around Colombian food in Bogotá, her father brought the traditional flavors of his Lebanese youth to their kitchen, which inspired Mariana to later fuse the two cuisines in her own cookbook, *Colombiana*, where this recipe was first published. We became immediate foodie friends, and I have followed Mariana's career as she built her Colombian hosting-ware business, Casa Velásquez (casavelasquez.co).

1  In a large bowl, combine the coconut, date syrup, tahini, anise seeds, and sesame seeds. Mix in the puffed millet with a large spatula until it's evenly coated in the coconut mixture—think Rice Krispies Treats. Using your hands, form the mixture into 10 to 12 golf ball–size spheres. If the mixture is too sticky, grease your hands with a touch of olive oil. Sprinkle with flaky salt.

2  Serve immediately on a platter or large plate, or store the alegrías in an airtight container at room temperature for up to a week or in the freezer for up to a month. Sometimes I like to eat them straight from the freezer!

These are great to bake over a long weekend or during the holidays, especially if you're looking to create a memorable homemade cookie to impress guests.

1  In the bowl of a stand mixer fitted with the paddle attachment or with a handheld mixer, beat the butter, tahini, confectioners' sugar, and vanilla on medium speed until smooth, for 2 to 3 minutes, scraping down the sides of the bowl as needed.

2  Add the flour, baking powder, and salt to the mixture and beat until just combined, about 1 minute.

3  Line two rimmed baking sheets with parchment paper.

4  Place the sesame seeds in a small bowl. Using your hands or a cookie scoop, roll heaping tablespoons of the dough into small balls (about 30g), and then roll each ball in the sesame seeds. Arrange the balls on the baking sheets, spacing them 1½ to 2 inches apart.

5  One by one, press your thumb into the center of each ball, creating a small indent to hold the filling. Refrigerate the dough for at least 30 minutes, or up to overnight. These cookies will be even better if you have time to freeze the portioned dough and bake from frozen.

6  When ready to bake, preheat the oven to 325°F.

7  Scoop about ½ teaspoon of the caramel sauce into the center of the cookies. The filling can be sticky, so you may need to use two spoons: one to scoop and one to scrape. You can also bake the cookies first, then add the caramel sauce once the cookies are slightly cooled gently re-creating the indent while the cookies are still warm.

8  Bake the cookies until browned around the edges, 14 to 16 minutes.

9  Remove the cookies from the oven and finish with a sprinkle of flaky salt over the caramel filling. Let the cookies cool for 10 minutes on the baking sheet, then use a metal spatula to transfer them to a wire rack to cool completely. Store the cookies in an airtight container at room temperature for up to a week.

# Triple Sesame Thumbprint Cookies

—

*Makes 14 cookies*
*Time: 45 minutes,*
*plus 30 minutes to chill*

½ cup (113g) unsalted butter, at room temperature

1 cup tahini

½ cup (65g) confectioners' sugar

½ teaspoon pure vanilla extract

1¼ cups (200g) all-purpose flour

1 teaspoon baking powder

1 teaspoon kosher salt

½ cup raw sesame seeds (I like to use a combination of black and white, but either is fine)

Tahini Salted Caramel Sauce (page 158)

Flaky salt, for garnish

# Brown Butter, Chocolate Chip & Halva Cookies

—

*Makes 16 cookies*

*Time: 20 minutes, plus overnight to rest, plus 14 minutes to bake*

¾ cup (170g) unsalted butter

½ cup (115g) tahini

⅓ cup (60g) packed light brown sugar

⅔ cup (140g) granulated sugar

1 egg plus 1 egg yolk, at room temperature

1 teaspoon pure vanilla extract

1¼ cups (200g) all-purpose flour

1 teaspoon baking soda

1 teaspoon kosher salt

1 cup toasted unsalted hazelnuts or walnuts, finely chopped (optional)

½ cup coarsely chopped 70% dark chocolate (see Note)

⅓ cup halva, crumbled into small pieces

½ teaspoon flaky salt

The first chocolate chip tahini cookie I made came from a recipe by an Atlanta-based Israeli chef and recipe developer, Danielle Oron. She was an early adopter of using tahini in sweet baking. Since then, I've tried countless versions, and I'm convinced that adding tahini is an absolute game-changing step. When it came to developing my own recipe, I was determined to keep improving upon what was already available. I wanted to create a cookie that felt like the ultimate trifecta of taste, texture, and that special "wow" factor that would convince you that all of the extra steps were worth the effort.

1   In a small saucepan, melt the butter over medium heat. When it begins to foam, lower the heat slightly so it doesn't burn and continue cooking for a few more minutes, until the butter has turned a deep golden brown and the milk solids have separated and settled at the bottom of the saucepan. Keep a close eye on the butter as it cooks so it doesn't burn—the butter will very quickly go from sizzling to silent once it's almost ready. Remove the browned butter from the heat and pour into a small bowl to cool slightly. Cover and refrigerate or freeze the browned butter until solidified, about 20 minutes.

2   Place the solidified browned butter in the bowl of a stand mixer fitted with the paddle attachment or a large bowl if using a handheld mixer. Add the tahini and beat until smooth on medium speed. Stop the mixer and scrape down the sides before adding both sugars and beating until combined.

3   Add the egg, egg yolk, and vanilla and beat on medium-high speed until fluffy, scraping down the sides of the bowl as needed, 3 to 4 minutes.

4   In a medium bowl, whisk the flour, baking soda, and kosher salt. Add the flour mixture to the dough and mix on low speed until the ingredients are well combined. Scrape the sides of the bowl one final time before folding in the hazelnuts (if using) and chocolate.

5   Line two rimmed baking sheets with parchment paper.

*Continued*

Brown Butter,
Chocolate Chip &
Halva Cookies

—

*continued*

6  Scoop golf ball–size portions of dough (about 50g) and place on the prepared baking sheets, allowing at least 1½ inches of space between each scoop. Transfer the baking sheet to the refrigerator and allow the dough to rest for at least 2 hours (or preferably overnight).

7  When ready to bake, preheat the oven to 350°F.

8  Place a small chunk of the halva in the center of each cookie and use your thumb to gently press it into the dough.

9  Bake until the edges are golden, about 14 minutes, rotating the baking sheets halfway through to ensure the cookies bake evenly. The cookies may look a little underdone in the center, but they will firm up as they cool.

10  Sprinkle the cookies with the sea salt while they are still warm, then use the mouth of a glass or a circular cookie cutter to rotate around each cookie to make the edges perfectly round (if that matters to you!).

11  The cookies are best eaten warm or on the day you bake them, but they can also be stored in an airtight container at room temperature for up to 3 days.

—

Note: *I prefer to use 70% dark chocolate. You may also use chocolate chips, but coarsely chopping the chocolate in larger pieces will give you decadent puddles of chocolate in the center of the cookie.*

There are countless chefs who have inspired my approach to cooking, but very few have had as profound of an influence as Yotam Ottolenghi. While tahini might be thousands of years old, Yotam was one of the first to bring this ancient ingredient to the forefront of culinary conversations and restaurant menus around the world. He embraced both its sweet and savory applications in creative ways that now seem more commonplace but at the time were highly innovative.

I was lucky to meet Yotam back in 2015 at the book signing for *Nopi*, a book he cowrote with Ramael Scully. My Seed + Mill cofounders, Monica, Lisa, and I, joined the long line to have our books signed and a photo taken with Yotam. At the time, our business was still just a "seed" of an idea. When we eventually launched the business, that picture with Yotam was the first picture we shared on our Instagram account.

I credit Yotam with creating the first version of a tahini-swirled brownie that served as inspiration for my own version: a brownie that can be baked in an ovenproof skillet and served directly from oven to table as a spectacular dessert centerpiece for a crowd.

1  Preheat the oven to 375°F (skip this step if you are making the batter a day in advance). Grease a 9-inch oven-safe skillet with butter or line a 13 by 9-inch baking pan with parchment paper.

2  Fill a saucepan or double boiler with about 1 inch of water and bring to a simmer over medium heat. Combine the butter and chocolate in a heatproof bowl set over the saucepan, making sure that the base of the bowl is not touching the water. Scrape down the sides of the bowl with a spatula so that the chocolate doesn't burn. Once melted, stir to combine, then set the bowl aside to allow the mixture to cool for a few minutes.

3  In the bowl of a stand mixer fitted with the paddle attachment or in a large bowl if using a handheld mixer, beat the eggs and sugar on medium speed until pale and creamy, 3 to 4 minutes.

4  Add the melted chocolate to the egg mixture and use a rubber spatula to gently fold together. Set aside.

# Tahini Skillet Brownie, Made for Sharing

—

*Serves up to 6 people from the skillet, or makes 12 square brownies*

*Time: 45 minutes*

9 tablespoons (127g) unsalted butter, cubed, plus more for the pan

9 ounces (255g) 70% dark chocolate, chopped

4 eggs, at room temperature

2¼ cups (450g) sugar

1 cup (125g) all-purpose flour

3 tablespoons cocoa powder (the best quality you can find)

½ teaspoon kosher salt

½ cup toasted walnuts, coarsely chopped (optional)

8 ounces halva, broken into 1-inch chunks (uneven pieces are fine)

7 to 8 tablespoons tahini, plus more for drizzling

1 teaspoon flaky salt

Ice cream for serving

*Continued*

5  Sift the flour, cocoa powder, and kosher salt into a large bowl, then add the chocolate mixture, walnuts, and halva. Gently stir with a rubber spatula until just combined.

6  Pour the batter into the prepared skillet and use a spatula to smooth over the top.

7  Dollop the tahini, 1 tablespoon at a time, into the batter in seven or eight spots spread across the skillet. Use a skewer, toothpick, or the back of a teaspoon to swirl the tahini dollops into various shapes to create a pretty pattern. Have fun—there's no right or wrong here!

8  If you're preparing these brownies in advance, refrigerate the skillet until ready to bake. (Remember to preheat the oven before baking if making the batter in advance.) Bake 25 to 30 minutes. Use a metal skewer to check for doneness: if you are planning to serve and eat the dish hot from the oven, the skewer does not need to come out completely clean. However, if you are making this to serve as cold brownie squares, bake until the skewer comes out clean. The baking time will depend on the size of your pan and the thickness of the batter, but I suggest checking for doneness from 25 minutes on.

9  If serving hot, transfer the skillet directly from the oven to the table, sprinkle with the flaky salt, and top with a few scoops of ice cream and an extra drizzle of tahini.

——

Note: *For a pro-entertaining move, make the batter up to 24 hours in advance, refrigerate, then simply pop the skillet into a hot oven when you're ready to bake. If you are planning to make this recipe as cold brownie squares, add the sea salt when the brownies are warm and just out of the oven and omit the additional drizzle of tahini. Store in an airtight container at room temperature for up to a week.*

I grew up eating rocky road, a chocolate bark of sorts that's popular in Australia. It is typically made by mixing melted chocolate with marshmallows, gummy candies, and nuts, then sliced into cubes once set. It was my dad's favorite treat, and I proudly watched him embrace his late-stage interest in cooking by teaching himself how to make rocky road (in part to satisfy his own sweet tooth but more likely to impress his grandkids). Oh, Dad, how I wish you were still here to recipe test my Middle Eastern take on your favorite Aussie classic.

1  Line a 5 by 9-inch loaf pan or 8-inch square baking pan with plastic wrap with enough overhang to cover the pan.

2  Fill a saucepan or double boiler with about 1 inch of water and bring to a simmer over medium heat. Place the chocolate in a heat-safe bowl set over the pan, making sure that the base of the bowl is not touching the water. Melt the chocolate, stirring until smooth. Stir in the tahini and set aside.

3  In a large bowl, combine the macadamia nuts, Turkish delight, and halva, then pour in the melted chocolate. Use a rubber spatula to gently combine and coat all the add-ins.

4  Pour the mixture into the prepared pan and top with the Sweet Dukkah (if using).

5  Use the plastic wrap overhang to cover the pan and refrigerate until firm, at least 1 hour. Remove the rocky road from the loaf pan and slice into bars or squares. Rocky Road will last in an airtight container in the refrigerator for up to 1 month.

# Rocky Road: An Ode to My Dad's Favorite Treat

—

*Makes 10 to 15 pieces*
*Time: 15 minutes,*
*plus at least 1 hour to set*

2 cups semisweet chocolate chips

½ cup tahini

1 cup macadamia nuts or peanuts

1 cup store-bought Turkish delight or another gummy candy (see Note)

8 ounces halva, cut into 1-inch cubes

2 tablespoons Sweet Dukkah (page 56; optional)

—

**Note:** *You can also swap the Turkish delight or gummy candies for a combination of pretzels, popcorn, dried fruit, coconut flakes, or whatever you have in your pantry that day!*

# Sesame & Miso Peach Crumble

—

*Serves 6*
*Time: 1 hour and 15 minutes*

6 to 7 unpeeled ripe peaches (2½ pounds), pitted, and sliced into ¼-inch wedges

Zest and juice of 1 lemon

1½ tablespoons light brown sugar

1 teaspoon cornstarch

1 tablespoon water

1 cup all-purpose flour

1 cup granulated sugar

½ cup walnuts, coarsely chopped

½ cup (1 stick) unsalted butter, melted

⅓ cup tahini

⅓ cup sesame seeds

1 tablespoon white miso

1¼ teaspoons kosher salt

1 teaspoon sesame oil

Ice cream or whipped cream for serving

My mum would make apple crumble for dessert almost every Friday night. She was very precise about her recipe, and I have vague memories of her disapproval whenever I would try to add other ingredients to her crumble topping. When I started a family of my own, I continued the tradition of making fruit crumbles, but I was less focused on following a recipe and more excited to empty my pantry of whatever seeds, nuts, sugars, and flours that I happened to have on hand that week. I always mix the crumble by hand, tasting as I go, until I achieve a texture that's somewhere in between not-too-dry and sandy and not-too-wet and soggy! I recently started adding miso to my crumble, which I think adds a unique depth of flavor and a whole new expression to this nostalgic dessert.

1  Preheat the oven to 375°F.

2  In a 9-inch or 8-inch square or round baking dish, toss the peaches with the lemon zest, lemon juice, and brown sugar (if using).

3  In a small bowl, whisk the cornstarch and water. Add the mixture to the peaches, toss gently to combine, and set aside.

4  In a medium bowl, combine the flour, granulated sugar, walnuts, butter, tahini, sesame seeds, miso, salt, and sesame oil. Using your hands or a fork, mix until just incorporated and the mixture looks like wet sand but holds together when pressed.

5  Crumble the topping over the peaches, squeezing some of the topping into larger chunks and letting some remain loose and crumbly.

6  Bake until the topping is golden brown and the peaches are fragrant and bubbling, about 1 hour. Check the crumble after about 30 minutes—if the topping seems to be burning, tent the baking pan with aluminum foil.

7  Serve warm with the ice cream or a dollop of whipped cream. The crumble can be made up to 2 days in advance and reheated in the oven covered with foil.

# Heavenly Halva Cake

—

*Recipe shared by*
Hanna Geller

*Serves 12*
*Time: 1 hour*

**For the crumble (see Note)**

3½ ounces halva, crumbled

3½ ounces 70% dark chocolate, finely chopped

2 ounces toasted pistachios, finely chopped

**For the cake**

10 tablespoons unsalted butter, plus more for greasing

1 cup granulated sugar

½ cup light brown sugar

3 eggs, at room temperature

1½ cups sour cream

1 teaspoon pure vanilla extract

2¼ cups all-purpose flour

1 teaspoon ground cinnamon

1 teaspoon ground cardamom

1 teaspoon baking soda

1 teaspoon baking powder

¾ teaspoon kosher salt

**For the tahini glaze**

1 cup confectioners' sugar

¼ cup whole milk

2 tablespoons tahini

2 tablespoons maple syrup

When people decry social media as the end of human connection and true friendship, I love to share the story of how I met Hanna—who after a chance, brief interaction on Instagram has now become not only a dear friend but also a professional collaborator and mentor. Hanna discovered Seed + Mill while wandering through Chelsea Market with her four sons. She posted a picture of our tahini soft serve with the caption "OMG. Best thing I have ever tasted. Seed + Mill, when are you coming to London?" Little did Hanna know how much I wanted our tahini and halva to be enjoyed on the other side of the Atlantic. With her boundless enthusiasm, Hanna made that happen for us, opening our first account in London at the historic Panzer's Deli! In addition to running her recipe blog, Building Feasts, Hanna also hosts cooking classes and supper clubs in her London home.

1  Preheat the oven to 350°F. Liberally grease a 10-inch Bundt pan or a 13 by 9-inch rectangular pan with butter.

2  **Make the crumble:** In a small bowl, combine the halva, chocolate, and pistachios. Set aside.

3  **Make the cake:** In a stand mixer fitted with the paddle attachment, beat the butter, granulated sugar, and brown sugar on high speed until pale and fluffy, 3 to 5 minutes. Add the eggs, one at a time, scraping down the bowl with a flexible spatula as needed and beating well after each addition. Beat in the sour cream and vanilla.

4  In a medium bowl, combine the flour, cinnamon, cardamon, baking soda, baking powder, and salt.

5  Add the flour mixture to the batter and beat on low speed until just combined.

6  Pour half the batter into the prepared pan, sprinkle all but 2 tablespoons of the crumble over the top of the batter, then spoon in the remaining batter. Bake until a skewer comes out clean, 35 to 40 minutes.

7  Let the cake cool in the pan for 15 minutes, then invert onto a wire rack to cool completely.

8 **Make the tahini glaze:** In a small bowl, whisk the confectioners' sugar, milk, tahini, and maple syrup until smooth. Drizzle the glaze over the slightly warm cake and top with the reserved 2 tablespoons of crumble. The cake will keep in an airtight container at room temperature for up to 3 days.

*Note: Double or triple the crumble ingredients and store the extra crumble in your pantry to sprinkle over granola, overnight oats, or ice cream!*

# Benne Sandwich Wafers with Peanut Butter Filling

—

*Makes 14 wafers*
*Time: 1 hour*

**For the wafers**

½ cup (1 stick) cold unsalted butter, cubed

¾ cup light brown sugar

1 egg

½ teaspoon pure vanilla extract

½ teaspoon kosher salt

½ cup benne seeds (see Note)

½ cup all-purpose flour

¼ teaspoon baking soda

**For the filling**

½ cup (1 stick) unsalted butter, at room temperature

¼ cup smooth peanut butter

2 tablespoons tahini

⅓ cup confectioners' sugar

2 tablespoons milk of your choice

¾ teaspoon kosher salt

½ teaspoon pure vanilla extract

*Continued*

These delicate wafers are made with benne seeds, which are part of the same species as sesame and have virtually the same taste and texture. Benne seeds are believed to have been brought to the United States by West African slaves. They are an important element in the Gullah Geechee culinary tradition, which is the foundation of many Southern dishes, developed by slaves and their descendants in and around the Carolinas. My sister, Talia, now lives in North Carolina, and I first discovered the famous benne wafer cookie on a family trip we took to Charleston, where Gullah food is proudly celebrated.

1  **Make the wafers:** In a stand mixer fitted with the whisk attachment or with a handheld mixer, beat the butter and brown sugar on medium speed until pale and fluffy, about 3 minutes. Add the egg, vanilla, and salt and beat for 2 minutes more.

2  In a medium bowl, combine the benne seeds, flour, and baking soda. Add the flour mixture to the batter in the stand mixer and beat on medium speed until well combined, about 2 minutes. Cover and refrigerate the dough for 30 minutes.

3  When ready to bake, preheat the oven to 350°F and line two rimmed baking sheets with parchment paper.

4  Using a tablespoon, spoon out small balls of dough (about 30g each) and place them on the prepared baking sheets, leaving at least 2 inches of space between each ball. Use the back of a spoon to flatten the dough to about ¼ inch high.

5  Bake until golden, 9 to 10 minutes. The wafers will spread on the baking sheet, so use a circular cookie cutter or upturned cup to mold them into even circles while they're still warm. You may also want to use a metal spatula to gently flatten the cookies so they are all an even height.

6  Allow the wafers to cool on the baking sheet for 5 minutes before gently transferring them to a wire rack to cool completely. The wafers can be stored in an airtight container at room temperature until you're ready to add the filling.

7  **Make the filling:** In the bowl of a stand mixer fitted with the paddle attachment or with a handheld mixer, combine the butter, peanut butter, and tahini and beat on medium speed

until smooth, about 2 minutes. Add the confectioners' sugar, milk, salt, and vanilla and beat until very light and fluffy, about 3 minutes.

8  Spoon or pipe a thin layer of filling onto the base of each wafer and gently press a similar-size cookie on top. Serve the filled cookies within a few hours of filling. The filling can be made up to 3 days in advance and stored in the refrigerator. Bring to room temperature before using. Unfilled cookies will last in an airtight container at room temperature for up to 5 days.

Note: *Benne seeds are available online and at many specialty grocery stores or substitute them with well-toasted sesame seeds.*

I wrestled with making a great pavlova for years and realized (through many failed attempts) that this is not a moment for going "off-road" with quantities or temperatures. You need to follow the recipe precisely if you want this dessert to look as pictured. But the good news is that you can always turn an imperfect pavlova into an Eton mess (an equally delicious dessert for you to look up if you don't know it already!).

Top with cream and fruit, but given that pavlova is a dessert that thrives on contradiction, I prefer tart-flavored fruits and a tangy, creamy base such as labneh. Taking the contrasting flavors one step further, I added an earthy, slightly savory swirl of tahini to balance the sweet meringue.

1  Preheat the oven to 275°F. Line a rimmed baking sheet with parchment paper.

2  In a stand mixer fitted with the whisk attachment or with a handheld mixer, whip the egg whites, salt, and cream of tartar on high speed until medium-stiff peaks form, about 3 minutes.

3  Add the water slowly while continuing to whip the egg whites on low speed. With the mixer still running, slowly add the sugar, then increase the speed to high and whip until the mixture is glossy and stiff peaks form, 3 to 4 minutes more. Fold in the cornstarch, vanilla, and vinegar.

4  Spread the meringue over the prepared baking sheet in your preferred shape until it is about 1 inch high.

5  Drizzle the tahini over the meringue and gently use the back of a spoon to create a swirl pattern.

6  Bake until the meringue starts to turn a very pale color, 1 hour, then reduce the oven temperature to 250°F and continue to bake for 45 minutes. Turn off the oven (don't open the door), and allow the meringue to sit in the oven for at least 1 hour, or up to overnight. This slow cooling process is what will make the pavlova crispy on the outside and soft on the inside.

7  Top the pavlova with the labneh, fruit, and halva to serve. Eat immediately, as pavlova is best the day it is taken out of the oven!

# Tahini-Swirled Pavlova with Summer Fruit & Halva

—

*Serves 6 to 8*
*Time: 20 minutes,*
*plus 2 hours 45 minutes*
*in the oven*

5 egg whites, at room temperature

¼ teaspoon kosher salt

⅛ teaspoon cream of tartar

3 tablespoons cold water

1¼ cups superfine sugar

1 tablespoon cornstarch

1 teaspoon pure vanilla extract

1 teaspoon white vinegar

¼ cup tahini

1 cup labneh, crème fraîche, or plain Greek yogurt

1 cup fresh mixed berries, sliced peaches, or another fruit of your choice

½ cup crumbled halva

# Molly's Fairy Bread

—

*Serves 1*
*Time: 5 minutes*

1 to 2 tablespoons tahini

1 slice fresh or toasted challah or another bread of your choice

1 to 2 tablespoons rainbow sprinkles

If you don't already know about Molly Yeh, now is the time to start reading her blog, following her on social media, eating at her restaurant, Bernie's, buying one of her cookbooks, or watching her television show, *Girl Meets Farm*. Is there anything Molly can't do?!

I first discovered Molly when we started Seed + Mill and I was looking to connect with other tahini-obsessed foodies. A self-described tahini addict, Molly has a down-to-earth approach to food, cooking, and life that's been influenced by her Jewish and Chinese heritage, her transition from Juilliard-trained percussionist to recipe developer, and her eventual move from city to farm. When Molly published her first cookbook, I called her team and pitched what I (naively) thought was a brilliant idea for the book party: to fill a vintage bathtub with tahini and have Molly take a dip. Suffice to say her publicist didn't go for it!

Less of a recipe and more of an idea, fairy bread is commonly served at Australian kids' birthday parties and is typically made with buttered white bread and sprinkles. This version, made with challah in place of white bread and tahini in place of butter, is an homage to Molly's culturally layered identity. It's a great snack to make for kids after school or to feed our inner child on a weekend morning.

Spread the tahini over the bread and cover with the sprinkles. Enjoy immediately!

It's impossible not to feel joyful watching Zoë François in the kitchen—her energy, warmth, and creativity are infectious. On her blog, Zoë Bakes, she makes complex desserts look easy, offering thoughtful advice and gorgeous photos. Growing up, there was always a brick of halva in Zoë's fridge where the butter was supposed to be. In an otherwise sugar-free kitchen, Zoë's mom was somehow persuaded to make an exception for halva. Continuing with that tradition, Zoë now keeps a brick of halva in her own kitchen, nibbling on small slivers at a time to satisfy something deeper than just a craving for sweets.

This is a great cake to try for Passover gatherings since it's naturally gluten-free, but it also makes for a stunning dessert at any time of the year.

1  **Make the meringue layer:** Preheat the oven to 350°F. Generously grease a 16 by 12-inch baking sheet, then line it with greased parchment paper.

2  In a stand mixer fitted with the whisk attachment or with a handheld mixer, whip the egg whites, salt, and cream of tartar on medium-high speed until medium-stiff peaks form, about 3 minutes.

3  With the mixer on medium-low speed, drizzle in the water. Slowly sprinkle in the sugar a little at a time; this may take a minute or so. Increase the speed to high and whip the mixture until very stiff, glossy peaks form, about 5 minutes.

4  With a flexible spatula, gently fold the cornstarch, vanilla, and vinegar into the egg whites.

5  Evenly spread the meringue over the prepared baking sheet. Bake until it starts to turn a light caramel color, about 20 minutes. It will puff considerably while it bakes but will settle once it is out of the oven. Let the meringue cool completely on the baking sheet. Once cool, cover with a clean kitchen towel—the meringue can be stored this way for up to 1 day.

6  **Make the ganache:** In a small saucepan, bring the cream to a simmer over medium heat. Remove from the heat and add the chopped chocolate.

# Halva Diva Cake

—

*Recipe shared by*
*Zoë François*

*Serves 6 to 8*
*Time: 1 hour and 30 minutes,*
*plus 40 minutes rest time*

**For the meringue layer**

Butter, for greasing

5 egg whites, at room temperature

Pinch of kosher salt

⅛ teaspoon cream of tartar

3 tablespoons cold water

1¼ cups superfine sugar

1 tablespoon plus 1 teaspoon cornstarch

1 teaspoon pure vanilla extract

1 teaspoon white wine vinegar, apple cider vinegar, or distilled white vinegar

**For the chocolate ganache**

1 cup heavy cream

8 ounces 70% dark chocolate, finely chopped

**For the tahini buttercream**

¾ cup confectioners' sugar

½ cup (1 stick) unsalted butter, at room temperature

1 teaspoon kosher salt

*Continued*

## Halva Diva Cake

—

*continued*

1 teaspoon pure vanilla
extract

¼ cup tahini

**For assembly**

½ cup crumbled halva

1 cup pistachios,
finely chopped

7  Swirl the saucepan to submerge the chocolate. Let it sit for 3 minutes then gently whisk the mixture until smooth. Keep the ganache in the saucepan until ready to use.

8  **Assemble the cake:** Loosen the meringue from the baking sheet. Spread half the ganache over the top and sprinkle with the halva and all but 2 tablespoons of the pistachios. Refrigerate until the ganache is solid, about 20 minutes.

9  Meanwhile, **make the buttercream:** In the bowl of a stand mixer fitted with the paddle attachment or with a handheld mixer, beat the confectioners' sugar, butter, salt, and vanilla on medium speed until smooth.

10  With the mixer running, drizzle in the tahini and beat, stopping as necessary to scrape down the sides of the bowl, until a smooth, spreadable frosting forms. Use immediately.

11  Spread the buttercream over the chilled ganache. Refrigerate until the buttercream is firm, about 20 minutes.

12  Cover the cake with plastic wrap and invert it onto the back side of a second baking sheet. Remove the parchment from the bottom of the meringue and invert the cake again onto a cutting board (the buttercream layer should end up back on top). Cut the cake in half lengthwise and then in thirds crosswise, so you have six sections. Stack the sections. Use a knife dipped in hot water to clean up any straggly bits.

13  Pour the remaining ganache over the top of the cake and sprinkle with the remaining 2 tablespoons pistachios. Transfer to a plate and serve immediately. The cake will last in the refrigerator for up to 3 days but is best served at room temperature.

# Tahini Semifreddo with Seed & Nut Brittle

—

*Serves 6 to 8*

*Time: 25 minutes, plus 6 hours to freeze (or preferably overnight)*

Lots of people claim to have a second stomach when it comes to dessert. When it comes to ice cream, I seem to have a third. Even when I can't imagine another mouthful, I've always got room for something cold, sweet, and creamy. What I particularly love about this dessert is that I can make it a couple of days in advance and slice it at the table for easy, elegant entertaining. You can also scoop the semifreddo into cups or cones if you prefer. Consider going all out and serving this with a drizzle of Salted Tahini Caramel Sauce (page 158).

2 eggs plus 2 egg yolks

⅓ cup sugar

1 tablespoon honey or date syrup

1 teaspoon pure vanilla extract

1 teaspoon kosher salt

½ cup tahini

1½ cups heavy cream

1½ cups crumbled Seed & Nut Brittle (page 207), or 1 cup crumbled halva plus ½ cup chopped toasted almonds

Tahini Salted Caramel Sauce (page 158) for serving (optional)

1 Line a 9 by 5-inch loaf pan with plastic wrap, leaving at least 3 inches of overhang on either side to cover the semifreddo later on. If making the semifreddo well in advance, use a double layer of plastic wrap here to protect the semifreddo against unwanted freezer smells.

2 Fill a saucepan or double boiler with about 1 inch of water and bring to a simmer over medium heat. Combine the eggs, egg yolks, sugar, honey, vanilla, and salt in a large metal bowl and set the bowl over the simmering water, making sure the bottom of the bowl does not touch the water. Beat vigorously with a whisk or handheld mixer until the mixture is thick and pale, 2 to 3 minutes, then remove from the heat and continue beating vigorously until the mixture has cooled slightly, about 6 minutes. Use a flexible spatula to gently fold in the tahini until well incorporated. Set the bowl aside to continue cooling.

3 In a stand mixer fitted with the whisk attachment or with a handheld mixer, whip the cream until medium-stiff peaks form, about 3 minutes.

4 Give the cooled egg mixture a vigorous stir. With a flexible spatula and in two batches, gently fold the whipped cream into the egg mixture until the two mixtures are fully incorporated.

5 Pour half of the mixture into the prepared loaf pan, then sprinkle the top with ¾ cup of the seed brittle. Some of the brittle may sink, which is fine, but an even layer is the goal. Pour the remaining mixture into the loaf pan and scatter the remaining ¾ cup seed brittle over the top.

*Continued*

6  Cover the pan with the plastic wrap overhang and freeze for at least 6 hours (or preferably overnight) before serving. The semifreddo will last in the freezer for up to 1 month.

7  When ready to serve, use the plastic wrap overhang to lift the ice cream loaf from the pan and place it on a platter or cutting board.

8  To ensure smooth edges for your slices, dip a sharp knife in boiling water, then dry it completely before cutting the semifreddo into 2-inch slices. Drizzle the slices with the Salted Tahini Caramel Sauce, if desired.

Tahini Semifreddo
with Seed & Nut
Brittle

—

*continued*

This is an unconventional and decadent flavor twist on a classic bowl of ice cream that will linger on in your food memory bank for a while. The earthy, buttery, crispy sage meets sweet, flaky halva and creamy ice cream, creating an easy yet sophisticated finale to a meal. If serving for guests, I recommend crisping the sage and browning the butter in advance so everything can be assembled at the last minute.

1   In a small saucepan, melt the butter over medium heat. When the butter starts to foam, add the sage and cook, allowing the sage to crisp and the butter to turn a deep golden brown, 2 to 3 minutes. Watch the butter carefully so it doesn't burn. Set aside so the butter can cool slightly. If browning the butter and sage in advance, when ready to serve, reheat the mixture until it has a pourable consistency.

2   Add the ice cream to serving bowls. Sprinkle with the halva and top with a tablespoon of the sage-infused brown butter. Serve immediately.

# Brown Butter, Sage & Halva Sundae

—

*Serves 4*
*Time: 5 minutes*

3 tablespoons
salted butter

6 to 8 sage leaves

4 scoops high-quality
vanilla ice cream

4 ounces halva,
crumbled

# Salted Honey & Tahini Snacking Cake

—

*Makes one 9 by 5-inch cake*
*Time: 1 hour 30 minutes*

Honey cake is traditionally served during the Jewish New Year, with honey being a culinary metaphor for the sweetness we hope for in the year ahead. While I usually embrace the symbolism in food and the continuity of holiday rituals, I've always found honey cake kind of boring and never made it. So, in the spirit of holding on to a tradition but adapting it to be something I would *actually* look forward to eating, I created my own version, adding earthiness with the tahini and a sublime cream cheese frosting.

**For the cake**

1¾ cups (210g) all-purpose flour

1½ teaspoons baking powder

¼ teaspoon baking soda

¼ teaspoon kosher salt

1 cup (227g) salted butter, at room temperature

¾ cup (150g) granulated sugar

½ cup (115g) tahini

1½ teaspoons vanilla extract

⅓ cup (110g) honey

3 eggs, at room temperature

½ cup full-fat Greek yogurt

**For the tahini cream cheese frosting**

4 ounces cream cheese, at room temperature

2 tablespoons unsalted butter, at room temperature

1¾ cups confectioners' sugar

¼ cup tahini

1 teaspoon pure vanilla extract

¼ teaspoon kosher salt

1  **Make the cake:** Preheat the oven to 350°F. Grease a 9 by 5-inch loaf pan or line it with parchment paper.

2  In a medium bowl, sift together the flour, baking powder, baking soda, and salt. Set aside.

3  In a stand mixer fitted with the paddle attachment or with a handheld mixer, combine the butter, granulated sugar, tahini, and vanilla and beat on medium speed until pale and fluffy, about 2 minutes. Add the honey then the eggs, one at a time, scraping down the bowl with a flexible spatula as needed and beating well after each addition.

4  Pour half of the flour mixture into the butter mixture and use a flexible spatula to fold the two together until just combined. Fold in the yogurt, followed by the rest of the flour mixture and fold until just combined. Pour the batter into the prepared pan.

5  Bake for 15 minutes, then reduce the oven temperature to 325°F and bake until the top is golden and a skewer inserted into the center comes out clean, 25 minutes more. Cool the cake in the pan for 10 minutes, then remove from the pan and cool completely on a wire rack.

6  **Make the frosting:** In the bowl of a stand mixer fitted with the whisk attachment or with a handheld mixer, combine the cream cheese, butter, confectioners' sugar, tahini, vanilla, and salt. Beat on medium speed until well combined and fluffy, 2 to 3 minutes. Use immediately or cover and refrigerate until ready to use.

7  Decoratively swoosh the frosting over the top of the cooled cake and serve immediately. The cake will last in an airtight container in the refrigerator for up to 3 days.

# A Fun Variation: Spiced Apple & Honey-Filled Tahini Cupcakes

These cupcakes, featuring a surprise filling bursting with spiced apples, are great to bake with kids.

1  Preheat the oven to 350°F and line a 12-cup muffin tin with paper liners.

2  Prepare the cake batter and frosting from the Salted Honey & Tahini Snacking Cake (opposite).

3  Fill each paper liner about three-fourths of the way with the batter and bake until the top of each cupcake is golden and a skewer inserted into the center of one of the cupcakes comes out clean. Cool the cupcakes completely in the tin on a wire rack.

4  **Make the filling:** In a large skillet, melt the butter over medium heat. Add the apples, brown sugar, and cinnamon and cook, stirring frequently, until the apples start to soften, about 10 minutes.

5  While the apples are cooking, in a small bowl, combine the cornstarch and 1 tablespoon water and stir until a smooth paste forms. Gently stir the paste into the apple mixture and continue cooking until the mixture thickens slightly, 1 to 2 minutes. Stir in 1 to 2 tablespoons more water if the apple mixture seems dry.

6  Remove the apples from the heat and let cool completely. The apple mixture can be made up to 3 days in advance and stored in an airtight container in the refrigerator.

7  To assemble, use a sharp-edged spoon or small knife to scoop out a 1-inch hole in the center of each cooled cupcake. (Save the cupcake middles to snack on!)

8  Fill each cavity with 1 teaspoon of the cooled apple mixture, then top with the cream cheese frosting (recipe opposite).

**For the filling**

2 tablespoons unsalted butter

4 apples, peeled, cored, and diced

½ cup packed light brown sugar

1 teaspoon ground cinnamon

1 tablespoon cornstarch

1 tablespoon water, plus more as needed

——

Note: *To create a more elegant frosting, place the mixture into a resealable plastic bag, seal the top, cut a bottom corner, and squeeze away. An extra flourish of drizzled honey and toasted sesame seeds are the icing on the icing!*

Salted Honey & Tahini
Snacking Cake, page 198

Spiced Apple & Honey
Tahini Cupcakes, page 199

# Black Sesame & Orange Tuiles

—

*Recipe shared by*
David Lebovitz

*Makes 20*
*Time: 1 hour, plus 1 hour*
*to rest*

½ cup plus 2 tablespoons sugar

3 tablespoons unsalted butter, melted

Zest of 1 orange

3 tablespoons freshly squeezed orange juice

1 tablespoon sesame oil

¾ cup sliced almonds

¼ cup all-purpose flour

2 tablespoons white sesame seeds

1½ teaspoons black sesame seeds

—

**Note:** *Serve with ice cream or a dollop of crème fraîche for a very impressive dessert.*

Back in 2004, my friend Paul Allam opened a tiny bakery in Sydney called Bourke Street Bakery in a corner shop so small only three customers were allowed in at a time. Not long after the bakery opened, Paul's wife called me, wild with excitement, to share that David Lebovitz had visited the store. *Who is David Lebovitz?* I wondered. I quickly discovered that David was an acclaimed pastry chef, cookbook author, and one of the internet's first food bloggers. I immediately bought David's first cookbook, *Room for Dessert*, and now religiously read David's beloved newsletter each week, sharing in his joy of food and living in Paris.

I was thrilled to get to know David fifteen years later at a dinner in New York and asked if he might like to share a favorite sesame recipe for my book. These tuiles remind David of his early pastry chef days in San Francisco.

1  In a medium bowl, combine the sugar, butter, orange zest, orange juice, and sesame oil.

2  Stir in the almonds, flour, and white and black sesame seeds. Cover and let sit for 1 hour at room temperature. The batter can also be refrigerated for up to 24 hours and brought to room temperature before baking.

3  Preheat the oven to 375°F. Line a rimmed baking sheet with parchment paper. Place 1 tablespoon of the batter in six equally spaced places on the prepared baking sheet. Bake until the tuiles have just browned all the way to the center, 8 to 9 minutes, turning the baking sheet in the oven once if necessary to brown them evenly. They are ready when the batter has just browned all the way through to the center. Don't take them any further.

4  Set the baking sheet on a wire rack and let the tuiles sit until they're cool enough to handle but still pliable, 3 to 5 minutes (the tuiles will get squished it you try to handle them when they're hot). Work quickly to lift the tuiles one at a time and drape them over a rolling pin. If the tuiles cool too quickly and lose their pliability, return them to the oven on the baking sheet for 30 to 45 seconds to rewarm. If not serving immediately, allow the tuiles to cool completely on the rolling pin before storing in an airtight container for up to 5 days.

Note: *If you're short on time, you can omit the Seed & Nut Brittle, but it can be made well in advance and will definitely make a statement if you're serving this as part of a celebration.*

In the words of the beloved late Australian actress Olivia Newton John, I am "hopelessly devoted to you," with "you" being my favorite dessert: carrot cake. But I suspect I am not alone in feeling that the cake is just a vehicle for excessive amounts of delicious cream cheese frosting, which I've made the star of this recipe. The addition of pineapple to a carrot cake can polarize bakers, but it's the way my mum always made it, so I wanted to continue with her tradition. Adding tahini to the frosting gives it a unique depth of flavor and has become my own little "nonnegotiable" family tradition to pass along.

## Tahini Cream Cheese Frosting with Carrot Cake & Seed Brittle

—

*Serves 8 to 10*
*Time: 1 hour and 10 minutes*

1  **Make the cake:** Preheat the oven to 350°F. Liberally grease an 8-inch baking pan with 1 to 2 tablespoons vegetable oil. Tilt the baking pan and add the sesame seeds to the sides, rotating until the sides of the pan are evenly coated with the seeds.

2  In a large bowl, whisk the flour, baking soda, baking powder, cinnamon, salt, ginger, nutmeg, and cardamom. Stir in the coconut and walnuts and set aside.

3  In the bowl of a stand mixer fitted with the paddle attachment or with a handheld mixer, combine the eggs, granulated sugar, 1½ cups vegetable oil, and the vanilla and beat on medium speed until pale and fluffy, 5 to 6 minutes. Use a flexible spatula to scrape down the sides of the bowl, then add the carrots and pineapple and beat for 1 minute more.

4  Use the spatula to gently stir the flour mixture into the batter, mixing until just combined.

5  Pour the batter into the prepared pan and bake until a skewer inserted into the center of the cake comes out clean. Allow the cake to cool completely in the pan before inverting onto a plate or wire rack.

### For the cake

1½ cups vegetable oil, plus more for greasing

¼ cup sesame seeds

2 cups all-purpose flour

½ teaspoon baking soda

1½ teaspoons baking powder

1 teaspoon ground cinnamon

½ teaspoon kosher salt

¼ teaspoon ground ginger

¼ teaspoon freshly grated nutmeg

¼ teaspoon ground cardamom

¾ cup unsweetened coconut flakes

1 cup toasted walnuts, coarsely chopped

3 eggs, at room temperature

1¾ cups granulated sugar

1 teaspoon pure vanilla extract

2 cups finely grated or shredded carrots

1 cup canned crushed pineapple, drained

*Continued*

## Tahini Cream Cheese Frosting with Carrot Cake & Seed Brittle

—

*continued*

**Tahini cream cheese frosting**

8 ounces cream cheese, softened

¼ cup salted butter, at room temperature

2 cups confectioners' sugar

¼ cup tahini

1 teaspoon pure vanilla extract

¾ teaspoon kosher salt

Seed & Nut Brittle
(recipe follows)

6  **Make the frosting:** In the bowl of a stand mixer fitted with the paddle attachment or with a handheld mixer, combine the cream cheese, butter, confectioners' sugar, tahini, vanilla, and salt and beat on medium speed until well combined and fluffy, 5 to 6 minutes. (The frosting can be made up to 3 days in advance, then kept covered and stored in the refrigerator. Let it come to room temperature and give it a vigorous stir before using.)

7  Cover the top of the cake with a thick coating of the frosting and decorate with shards or finely crumbled pieces of Seed & Nut Brittle. The cake will last in an airtight container in the refrigerator for up to 4 days.

Sesame

# Seed & Nut Brittle

1  In a small saucepan, combine the sugar and water over low heat. Cook until the sugar is dissolved, swirling the pan—do not stir. Dip a pastry brush in the mixture and use it to wet down the sides of the saucepan, making sure there are no stray crystals of sugar that haven't been fully dissolved.

2  Once the sugar has dissolved, increase the heat to medium-high. Boil the syrup for about 10 minutes, or until it turns a deep golden color. Watch it carefully so that it doesn't burn.

3  While the sugar is boiling, line a rimmed baking sheet with parchment paper and spread the nuts and seeds in a single layer over the parchment. (I only used sesame seeds in the brittle at right.) Keep an additional piece of parchment paper handy.

4  When the syrup is done, give the saucepan a gentle swirl, then immediately pour the syrup over the nuts and seeds so that they're evenly covered. Use a metal spatula to quickly spread and smooth the mixture into an even layer—you don't want the caramel to harden before it's been spread! If it hardens too quickly, transfer the baking sheet to an oven set at 350°F and bake the mixture for a few minutes, until the caramel is malleable again and you can more easily spread it with the seeds and nuts.

5  As a variation to step 4, you can also spread the caramel over the parchment-lined baking sheet first, then immediately sprinkle on the nuts and seeds while the caramel is still hot.

6  Let the brittle cool and harden on the baking sheet at room temperature, 10 to 15 minutes. Once hardened, place the second piece of parchment paper over the top of the brittle and use a rolling pin to smash the brittle into small shards or a fine crumble, or use your hands to break the brittle into larger pieces. The brittle can be stored in an airtight container in the refrigerator for up to 2 weeks.

*Time: 20 minutes*

1½ cups sugar

½ cup water

¾ cup finely chopped toasted and unsalted nuts and/or seeds (such as sesame seeds, pistachios, pecans, pepitas, or sunflower seeds)

There are so many things I adore about making a fruit galette that I hardly know where to start! I've made variations of this dessert with a variety of fruit, depending on what's in season. I've even made a savory version with tomatoes (they're a fruit)! Feel free to use store-bought frozen pie dough if you're short on time, but know that making it from scratch is easier than you think, and the process can be quite meditative, too.

1 **Make the dough:** First, make sure you are working in a cool workspace—your work surface, hands, and kitchen should be as cool as possible, and keep your butter and flour in the fridge until you're ready to use them. In a medium bowl, combine the flour, salt, and sugar. Add the butter and quickly cut into the flour mixture, using your thumb to flatten out the butter in the palm of your hand, until the mixture resembles a coarse oatmeal.

2 Add the ice water and knead until incorporated, then transfer the dough to a cold work surface, kneading until the shaggy-looking dough just holds together in a ball. If the dough is crumbly when squeezed, add up to 2 tablespoons more ice water, a little at a time, and continue kneading until it holds together in a ball. Don't worry if there are flattened streaks of butter in the dough—this will create a nice flakiness to your finished galette.

3 Divide the dough into two balls, then flatten each one into a 1-inch-thick disc and loosely wrap in plastic wrap. Refrigerate the dough for at least 30 minutes, preferably overnight.

4 **Make the filling:** Place a rimmed baking sheet in the oven, then preheat the oven to 425°F.

5 In a medium bowl, combine the orange juice and granulated sugar. Add the rhubarb and strawberries and toss until well coated. Set aside.

6 Remove one disc of dough from the fridge and place on a floured work surface or between two pieces of parchment paper. Allow the dough to warm slightly, then roll it out into a circle about 16 inches wide. The edges do not need to be perfectly round—mine are often a jagged mess, but the galette

# Rhubarb & Strawberry Galette with Halva Cream

—

*Serves 4 to 6*
*Time: 1 hour,*
*plus 30 minutes to chill*

**For the dough**

2½ cups all-purpose flour, plus more for rolling

1 teaspoon kosher salt

1 teaspoon granulated sugar

1 cup (2 sticks) cold unsalted butter, diced into ½-inch cubes

¼ cup ice water, plus more as needed

**For the filling**

3 tablespoons freshly squeezed or store-bought orange juice

3 tablespoons granulated sugar

¾ pound rhubarb (about 4 large stalks), trimmed and cut into 3-inch pieces

2 cups chopped strawberries

2 tablespoons tahini

3 tablespoons almond meal

1 tablespoon all-purpose flour

1 egg, lightly beaten

1 tablespoon raw or Demerara sugar

1 tablespoon untoasted sesame seeds

*Continued*

## Rhubarb & Strawberry Galette with Halva Cream

——

*continued*

**For the halva cream**

2 cups heavy cream

4 ounces halva, crumbled

will still look and taste delicious once baked. If using a floured work surface, transfer the dough to a piece of parchment paper once rolled.

7   Using a pastry brush or the back of a spoon, paint the tahini over the rolled dough, leaving a 1½-inch border. Scatter the almond meal evenly over the tahini.

8   Add the flour to the rhubarb mixture, gently toss to combine, then pile it over the almond meal (the layer of tahini and almond meal will absorb the extra fruit juices and add a delicious nutty flavor). The fruit will cook down, so pile it up about 2 inches high.

9   Fold the border of the dough toward the center, allowing the edges to overlap. Brush the top of the dough edges with the egg and sprinkle with the raw sugar and sesame seeds.

10   Remove the preheated baking sheet from the oven and place the galette with the parchment paper onto the baking sheet. Immediately return the baking sheet to the oven and lower the temperature to 375°F. Bake for 30 to 40 minutes, until the crust is golden brown and the fruit is starting to bubble. If the crust starts to get too brown, cover the edges with aluminum foil and continue baking.

11   While the galette is baking, in a stand mixer fitted with the whisk attachment or in a large bowl with a handheld mixer, whip the cream until soft peaks form. Fold in the halva with a flexible spatula.

12   Serve the galette warm or at room temperature with a spoonful of the halva cream. The galette will last in an airtight container in the refrigerator for up to 2 days.

——

Note: *This recipe makes enough dough for two galettes, so you can keep one disc of dough in the freezer for up to 3 months to use for future spontaneous entertaining!*

This cheesecake is perfect for a hot weekend when you don't want to turn the oven on but want a showstopping sweet treat for the center of your table. Browning your butter to make the base is not essential and you can use regular melted butter in a pinch, but if you don't agree that the smell of browned butter isn't the most delicious aroma in the world, then I'm not quite sure we can be foodie friends!

# Frozen Pistachio Halva Cheesecake

—

*Serves 8 to 10*
*Time: 25 minutes,*
*plus 6 hours to freeze*

1  **Make the base:** Line the bottom of a 9-inch springform pan with parchment paper.

2  In a food processor, pulse the biscuits to a fine crumb, then add the pistachios and salt and pulse a couple of times more until just combined. This allows the base to retain a crunchy texture—keep pulsing if you prefer a finer crumb. Transfer the mixture to a medium bowl.

3  Set a small heavy saucepan over medium heat. Add the butter and swirl to coat the bottom of the pan. After about 2 minutes, when the butter is just past melting, it will start to foam and then settle into a clear-ish golden liquid with brown specks (which are the milk solids browning and separating from the fat in the butter).

4  Pour the brown butter into the bowl with the biscuit mixture and use your hands or a spoon to combine until the mixture resembles wet sand and just holds together in your hand.

5  Spread the mixture over the bottom of the prepared pan, using the bottom of a glass or measuring cup to press it down into an even, smooth layer all the way to the pan's edges. I usually allow a little bit of the mixture to creep up the sides of the pan by half an inch.

6  **Make the filling:** In a stand mixer fitted with the paddle attachment or in a large bowl with a handheld mixer, beat the cream cheese, confectioners' sugar, and vanilla on medium speed until well combined, about 2 minutes. Scrape down the sides of the bowl with a flexible spatula, add the tahini, and beat again for 1 minute more.

### For the base

2¼ cups digestive biscuits (I like McVitie's) or plain graham crackers

1 cup lightly toasted pistachios

1 teaspoon kosher salt

6 tablespoons unsalted butter

### For the fillings & toppings

27 ounces (750g) cream cheese, at room temperature

¾ cup confectioners' sugar

1½ teaspoons pure vanilla extract

½ cup tahini

1½ cups heavy cream

8 ounces crumbled halva, plus 2 to 3 tablespoons

1 cup lightly toasted pistachios, finely chopped in a food processor

*Continued*

Frozen Pistachio
Halva Cheesecake

—

*continued*

7  In a medium bowl, whip the cream with a whisk until soft peaks form, 2 to 3 minutes. Fold half of the whipped cream into the cream cheese mixture until just incorporated. Gently fold in the rest of the whipped cream until the mixture is combined.

8  Pour half of the filling over the biscuit base. Sprinkle the 8 ounces halva and all but 3 tablespoons of the pistachios over the filling. Pour the remaining filling over the top and smooth the surface.

9  Cover the cake with plastic wrap and freeze for at least 6 hours or overnight.

10  At least 10 minutes before serving, remove the cake from the freezer to soften slightly. When ready to serve, loosen the cake by running a knife along the side of the pan, then remove the ring and place the cake on a serving dish. Scatter the remaining 2 to 3 tablespoons halva and 3 tablespoons pistachios over the cake.

11  To serve, dip a knife in boiling water, wipe it dry, and slice the cake, cleaning the knife between each cut. Once defrosted, the cake will last loosely covered in the refrigerator for up to 3 days, though it may lose its shape.

Maura is the pastry chef and co-owner of a group of bakeries and restaurants in and around Cambridge, Massachusetts. Her Middle Eastern bakery, Sofra, is one of those iconic spots that you simply cannot miss. I first discovered Maura at a cooking class she was teaching at a food conference I was attending. The conference organizers mentioned that one of the bakers needed tahini for her demo and asked if we could supply it. I popped in to join the class and was completely starstruck. Maura works with a quiet, humble confidence, creating beautifully presented food inspired by her travels and love of the food of the Middle East. This chocolate tart is sweet but not too sweet and was unanimously declared the team's favorite dessert during our photo shoot for this book.

1 **Make the cookie crust:** Grease a 9-inch tart pan with a removable bottom. In the bowl of a food processor, pulse the cookies until they're ground into fine crumbs. Transfer the ground cookies to a medium bowl and pour in the butter. Toss to coat and stir in the sesame seeds and salt.

2 Pour the crumb mixture into the prepared pan. Use the base of a glass or measuring cup to press the mixture firmly against the bottom and sides of the pan. You'll want the crust to be about ⅛ inch thick on the sides of the pan, with a thicker crumb across the bottom of the shell to support the tart. Freeze the crust for at least 1 hour or up to overnight.

3 When ready to bake, preheat the oven to 350°F. Place the chilled crust on a rimmed baking sheet. Bake until crisp, 10 to 12 minutes. Set aside to cool.

4 **Make the ganache:** In a medium bowl, combine the chocolate, tahini, and salt.

5 In a small saucepan, combine the cream and honey and cook over medium heat until the cream starts to bubble slightly at the edges but does not boil. Remove the saucepan from the heat and pour the cream mixture over the chocolate mixture. Let sit for 3 to 4 minutes to melt the chocolate, then stir well until the ganache is smooth and shiny. Immediately pour the ganache into the cooled crust. Let the tart sit at room temperature for 5 minutes before placing in the refrigerator, loosely covered,

# Bittersweet Chocolate Tahini Tart

—

*Recipe shared by*
Maura Kilpatrick

*Serves 8 to 10*
*Time: 30 minutes,*
*plus 5 hours to chill*

**For the cookie crust**

24 to 30 chocolate wafer cookies or chocolate graham crackers, or 2½ cups chocolate cookie crumbles (see Note)

3 tablespoons unsalted butter, melted

2 tablespoons sesame seeds

½ teaspoon kosher salt

**For the ganache**

8½ ounces bittersweet chocolate, coarsely chopped

5 tablespoons tahini

½ teaspoon kosher salt

1½ cups heavy cream

3 tablespoons honey

**For the halva whipped cream**

1 pound sesame halva

¾ cup heavy cream

*Continued*

Something Sweet

Bittersweet
Chocolate
Tahini Tart

——

*continued*

——

Note: *Oreo cookie crumbles work well in this recipe and are available on Amazon.*

to chill—this will keep the ganache shiny. Refrigerate until firm, 3 to 4 hours. The tart can be prepared up to 3 days in advance and refrigerated, loosely covered, until ready to serve.

6  **Make the halva whipped cream:** Break the halva into small pieces. In a medium saucepan, combine the halva and cream over medium heat and whisk until the halva has dissolved into the cream.

7  Remove the saucepan from the heat, transfer the halva cream to an airtight container, and refrigerate for at least 4 hours or up to overnight.

8  In a stand mixer fitted with the whisk attachment or with a handheld mixer, whip the chilled halva cream until very soft peaks form, 2 to 3 minutes.

9  When ready to serve, spoon the halva whipped cream over the top of the tart (I like to leave a 1-inch border so the ganache is visible).

10  To serve, dip a knife in boiling water, wipe it dry, and slice the tart into wedges, cleaning the knife between each cut. The tart will last loosely covered in the refrigerator for up to 4 days.

# Thank You

If I'd told thirty-eight-year-old me that within ten years I'd be living in New York, leading a beloved food company, and writing a cookbook, I would never have believed her. This book is a testament to the fact that dreams sometimes do come true. But this dream certainly didn't come true without remarkable contributions from countless others, for whom I am profoundly grateful:

My agent, **Leigh Eisenman**, for seeing my vision and relentlessly pushing me to write this book.

**Dervla Kelly**, your early encouragement paved the way for this book to become a reality. **Cristina Garces, Emma Campion**, and the entire Ten Speed Press team, including **Jane Chinn, Terry Deal, Clare Ling, Miriam Garron, Brianne Sperber**, and **Natalie Yera-Campbell** for your patience and faith in this project, and for giving me this precious opportunity to share my story.

**Maren Ellingboe King**, for your diligent recipe testing, moral support, and thoughtful edits.

**Alan Benson**, an incredibly talented photographer and master of light, who brought endless kindness, energy, and good humor to our shoot. A true mensch! **Emma Knowles**, food and prop stylist extraordinaire, for your friendship and hugs, and for bringing beauty to every image. **Jimmy, Ariella, Evelina, Nicola**, and **Shawan**, my dream team of prep cooks, hand models, and DJs, who made our photoshoot a career highlight! **Evelina**, for your beautiful illustrations and generous spirit. **Dan Perez**, for your stunning photos taken in the sesame fields.

My group of foodie girlfriends: Ivy, Anna, Susan, Amanda, Ronit, Danielle F., Danielle L., Gemma, Giselle, Sari, Shoshana, Jody, Michelle, and Jane, who bring laughter and joy to my life, and who each, in their own way, helped me give birth to this book.

Lisa and Monica, for your brilliant foresight and partnership in bringing Seed + Mill to life—thank you for giving me this chance to fulfill a bucket list dream.

The entire Seed + Mill team (current and former), for so passionately representing our brand and working by my side day in and day out.

The contributors (some of whom are pictured below) who generously shared their recipes and friendship: Ayesha Nurdjaja, Molly Yeh, David Lebovitz, Mariana Velásquez, Jamie Wei, Mona Talbott, Hanna Geller, Lior Lev Sercarz, Kenshiro Uki, Kristin Nelson, Kristina Costa, Maura Kilpatrick, Sylvie Charles, and Nisha Vora.

My mum, Jane, and sister, Talia, my first cooking teacher and first kitchen buddy, respectively. My heart aches that we have spent so many years living in different cities, but we've managed to create some spectacular memories in kitchens all over the world.

My children, Oliver and Annika: Cooking for you and your dad is both my greatest pleasure and my happiest place.

My husband, Chris, for your bottomless pit of patience, humility, good humor, and dishwashing skills. We've grown up, traveled, and built a life together spanning nearly thirty years. I'm quite honestly lost for words trying to express my love and gratitude for you.

Finally, this book only exists because of the wonderful group of Seed + Mill customers and community: I am infinitely grateful to be part of your daily meals and family celebrations. I am so proud that this book is in your hands!

# Index

Ten Speed Press
An imprint of the Crown Publishing Group
A division of Penguin Random House LLC
tenspeed.com

Typefaces: Cyreal's Lora, Perfectype's Qattico, and Adobe's Work Sans

Library of Congress Cataloging-in-Publication Data is on file with
the publisher.

Hardcover ISBN: 978-1-9848-6363-8
Ebook ISBN: 978-1-9848-6364-5

Manufactured in China

Editor: Cristina Garces | Production editor: Terry Deal
Designer: Emma Campion | Production designer: Mari Gill
Production and prepress color manager: Jane Chinn
Copyeditors: Terry Deal and Monika Dziamka
Proofreaders: Clare Ling and Miriam Garron
Indexer: Elizabeth T. Parson
Publicist: Natalie Yera-Campbell | Marketer: Brianne Sperber

10 9 8 7 6 5 4 3 2 1

First Edition